SAMS
Teach Yourself
MICROSOFT®
FRONTPAGE® 2000

Galen Grimes

in 10 Minutes

SAMS

A Division of Macmillan Computer Publishing
201 West 103rd St., Indianapolis, Indiana, 46290 USA

Sams Teach Yourself Microsoft® FrontPage® 2000 in 10 Minutes

Copyright © 1999 by Sams Publishing

International Standard Book Number: 0-672-31498-3

Library of Congress Catalog Card Number: 98-87799

Printed in the United States of America

First Printing: May 1999

01   00   4   3   2

Trademarks

Warning and Disclaimer

Executive Editor
Mark Taber

Acquisitions Editor
Randi Roger

Development Editor
Scott D. Meyers

Managing Editor
Lisa Wilson

Project Editor
Carol L. Bowers

Copy Editor
Patricia Kinyon

Indexer
Eric Schroeder

Proofreader
Kim Cofer

Technical Editor
Gina Carillo

Interior Design
Gary Adair

Cover Design
Aren Howell

Layout Technicians
Brandon Allen
Stacey DeRome
Susan Geiselman
Timothy Osborn
Staci Somers

CONTENTS

ABOUT THE AUTHOR

Galen A. Grimes has been working with computers since 1980 when he purchased his first PC, an Apple II+. Since then he has worked on PCs using DOS, Windows (3.1/95/NT 4.0), and UNIX and has programmed in about a dozen different programming languages including C/C++, Assembler, Pascal, BASIC, and Xbase. Galen has a master's degree in Information Science from the University of Pittsburgh and is currently a computer systems project manager at Mellon Bank in Pittsburgh, PA.

Galen has worked as an author for several Macmillan Computer Publishing divisions for the past six years and has written *Sams Teach Yourself Upgrading and Fixing PCs in 24 Hours, 10 Minute Guide to PC Upgrades, Sams Teach Yourself Netscape Communicator in 24 Hours, 10 Minute Guide to Netscape With Windows 95, 10 Minute Guide to the Internet With Windows 95, 10 Minute Guide to Novell NetWare, 10 Minute Guide to Lotus Improv, First Book of DR DOS 6,* and *10 Minute Guide to the Internet and World Wide Web,* second and third editions.

Although originally born and raised in Texas, Galen makes his home now in a quiet, heavily wooded section of Monroeville, PA, a suburb of Pittsburgh, with his wife Joanne and an assortment of deer, raccoons, squirrels, chipmunks, possums, groundhogs, and birds, which are all fed from their back door. Besides working with computers and surfing the Internet, Galen also spends his time playing golf, bicycling, dabbling in amateur astronomy, gardening, cooking, and refining the art of "couch-potatoing." Each fall, he and his wife Joanne are transformed into two of the most enthusiastic football fans for Penn State's Nittany Lions (see http://www.psu.edu/sports).

Galen can be reached either by email at galen@felixnet.com or through his Web site at http://www.felixnet.com.

DEDICATION

To my wife Joanne, who continues to provide me with both the inspiration and free time necessary to write.

ACKNOWLEDGMENTS

Special thanks to the book building team at Macmillan, which includes Amy Patton, Scott Meyers, Carol Bowers, Pat Kinyon, and Gina Carillo.

None of this would have been possible without their long hours and unending patience.

And a very special thanks to Randi Roger for her diligent efforts and tireless work in keeping this book on track and on schedule.

TELL US WHAT YOU THINK!

As the reader of this book, *you* are our most important critic and commentator. We value your opinion and want to know what we're doing right, what we could do better, what areas you'd like to see us publish in, and any other words of wisdom you're willing to pass our way.

You can fax, email, or write me directly to let me know what you did or didn't like about this book—as well as what we can do to make our books stronger.

Please note that I cannot help you with technical problems related to the topic of this book, and that due to the high volume of mail I receive, I might not be able to reply to every message.

When you write, please be sure to include this book's title and author as well as your name and phone or fax number. I will carefully review your comments and share them with the author and editors who worked on the book.

Fax: 317-581-4770

Email: `office_sams@mcp.com`

Mail: Mark Taber
          Associate Publisher
          Sams Publishing
          201 West 103rd Street
          Indianapolis, IN 46290 USA

INTRODUCTION

Everyone is always looking for a better way to perform a specific task. If the task you are looking to perform involves creating and managing a Web site, you need to be looking at FrontPage 2000. Regardless of whether you are building a simple personal Web site to show off the photos from last summer's vacation or you're in charge of a Web-based technical support site for a Fortune 500 company, FrontPage can fill the bill.

FrontPage enables you to use both simple and sophisticated HTML creation and editing tools in developing your site. It also includes all the tools you will later need to both publish and manage your site.

WELCOME TO *SAMS TEACH YOURSELF MICROSOFT FRONTPAGE 2000 IN 10 MINUTES*

Sams Teach Yourself Microsoft FrontPage 2000 in 10 Minutes takes a straightforward approach to guiding you through all the basic aspects of using a Web creation and management tool.

Sams Teach Yourself Microsoft FrontPage 2000 in 10 Minutes is for anyone who

- Is just learning to use HTML to create a Web site
- Wants to learn how to use FrontPage 2000
- Is looking for a new or different HTML editor and site management utility

HOW TO USE THIS BOOK

In addition to helping you learn how to use FrontPage 2000 to create and manage your Web site, this book also offers a broad range of helpful information and tips you can use while working on your Web site. You should use as many of the lessons as are applicable to the features you are including in your site. You should also keep this book handy as a resource and reference while you're learning FrontPage 2000 and while you're working on your site. You may not have to read it cover-to-cover; but keep in mind that even though you may not be using a particular feature in the site you are currently working on or the next site you are planning, a month from now or six months from now you may need to use one of the features you skip over now.

LESSON 1

INTRODUCTION TO FRONTPAGE 2000

In this lesson, you learn some of the fundamental concepts about using and working in FrontPage 2000.

UNDERSTANDING FRONTPAGE 2000, WEBS, AND HTML FILES

The World Wide Web continues to garner a vast amount of interest as more and more people start to view it not just as a novelty but as a useful tool for gathering news and information. National and world events continue to lure more users to the Internet and, after a while, some of these users will want to stop being "spectators" and will want to become "participants."

The World Wide Web, also referred to simply as "the Web" or WWW for short, continues to be the easiest and cheapest means of reaching a worldwide audience of millions. Most Internet service providers will provide the platform—all you need do is supply the content.

Let me take a moment to explain. Most of you reading this book, whether you know it or not, probably have access to a Web server from the person or persons providing you access to the Internet. If you are paying a monthly fee (the average is about $20) for Internet access, part of your package likely includes anywhere from 5–20MB of storage space on your provider's Web server for personal Web sites. Commercial host providers often provide upwards of 50–200MB of space for corporate Web sites.

This is your platform to the world! What you need now is the means to utilize your platform.

If you're still having a little trouble with the concept, here's another way to look at it. Imagine you have been given access to a 50,000-watt radio station but haven't clue about programming. In fact, you don't even know how to turn on the microphones. What this book is going to do is the equivalent of teaching you how to get your programs on the air.

FRONTPAGE AS HTML EDITOR, SITE MANAGEMENT TOOL, AND PUBLISHER

You will need several tools to produce your site on the WWW. You need space on your service provider's Web server and, of course, you'll need access to the Internet. The major tool you will use is FrontPage 2000, or simply FrontPage for short.

FrontPage will function as several tools in one:

- As a Web page creation tool
- As a Web site management tool
- As a Web site publishing tool

As a Web page creation tool, you will use the FrontPage editor to construct each page in your Web site. Your pages will be individual HTML files.

 HTML   Short for Hypertext Markup Language, HTML is "a markup language that is a subset of SGML and is used to create hypertext and hypermedia documents on the World Wide Web, incorporating text, graphics, sound, video, and hyperlinks."

HTML files are simple text files. They contain the actual text that you want to display onscreen, and they contain the coding for how your text and graphics are displayed on each Web page. Your HTML files also contain the coding for *links* to other Web pages.

 Links   These are hypertext connections inserted in a Web page that connect one Web page to a file or another Web page.

Figure 1.1 is an example of HTML coding, and Figure 1.2 is the same page displayed by a Web browser.

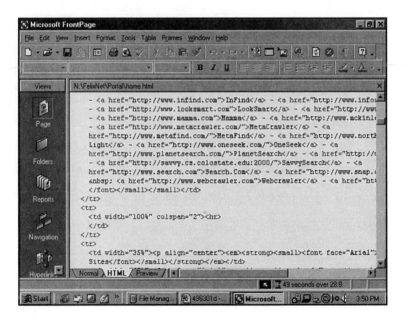

FIGURE 1.1   An example Web page in its native HTML format.

FrontPage is a WYSIWYG (What You See Is What You Get) type editor, meaning that you will actually see on your screen what your page looks like as you are creating it (see Figure 1.3), and how it will look when your page is published on the Web. The majority of this book is aimed at teaching you how to use FrontPage to create your Web pages.

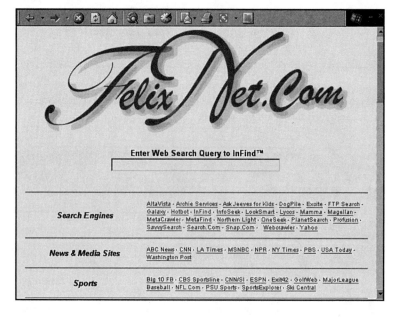

FIGURE 1.2   The same HTML page displayed by a Web browser.

As a Web site management tool, you will use FrontPage to assemble your collection of Web pages into a coherent Web site. This is what is known in FrontPage as a "Web." FrontPage will not only assemble your pages into a Web, it will also diagram how the pages interconnect in your Web (see Figure 1.4) and check the links in your Web to make sure they are all valid.

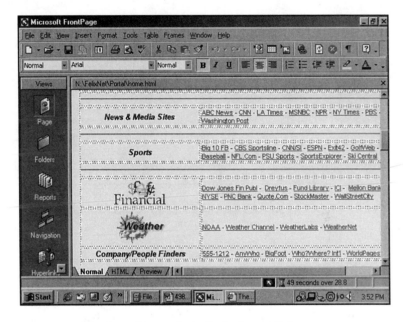

FIGURE 1.3   The FrontPage editor displaying a Web page as you create it.

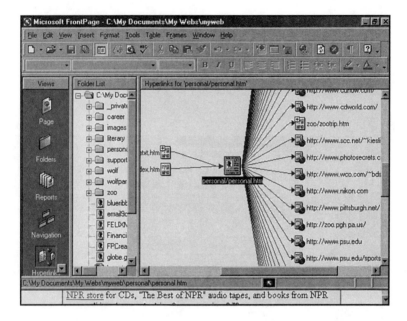

FIGURE **1.4**   A typical Web diagram in a FrontPage Web showing the interconnection of pages and images.

Finally, as a Web publishing tool, you will use FrontPage to transfer or publish your Web to the server where it will be seen on the Internet.

FrontPage makes the task of publishing your Web as easy as creating your Web. Publishing your Web is literally one-button simple. When you select the Publish Web command, FrontPage will establish a connection to the Web server where your Web will be published (see Figure 1.5), upload (copy) your Web to the server and even re-create, if necessary, the directory structure you constructed when you created your Web.

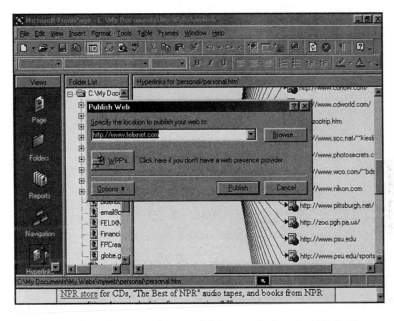

FIGURE 1.5   FrontPage ready to publish to a designated Web site.

In the lesson, you learned the gist of how you will use FrontPage to construct your Web site. If it sounds easy, that's because it is, or I should say will be. In the next lesson, you begin working with FrontPage by first learning how to install the program.

LESSON 2

INSTALLING FRONTPAGE 2000 AND WEB SITE BASICS

In this lesson, you learn how to install FrontPage 2000 on your PC.

INSTALLING FRONTPAGE 2000 ON YOUR PC

Installing FrontPage on your PC is relatively easy and should take you only a few minutes. FrontPage requires that you are at least running Windows 95/98. You can also install FrontPage on a PC running Windows NT. While FrontPage is mostly compatible with Microsoft Internet Explorer version 3.0 and later, some features do require IE 4.0 or later. If you are running Netscape, you should be using at least version 4.0 or later.

If you have already installed Microsoft Office 2000 you might already have FrontPage installed. If you purchased the standalone version of FrontPage 2000, or if FrontPage was not installed during the installation of Office 2000, then you need to install it. Here's what you need to do to install FrontPage 2000:

1. Insert your FrontPage CD-ROM in your CD-ROM drive.

2. If you do not have the Autorun CD feature turned on, from the Start menu, select Run and type *X*:\SETUP, where *X*:\ is the drive letter of your CD-ROM drive. In a few seconds, you will see the setup opening screen (see Figure 2.1).

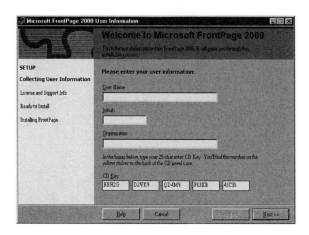

FIGURE 2.1   The FrontPage setup opening screen.

3. Enter the requested information in the opening screen (see
Figure 2.2) and select Next>>to continue.

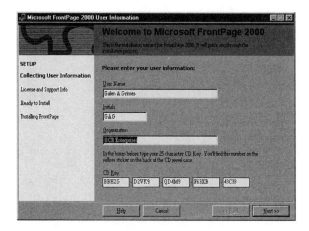

FIGURE 2.2   Entering your personal information into FrontPage
setup.

4. The next screen is the license agreement (see Figure 2.3). Read
the agreement and select I accept the Terms in the License
Agreementand then select Next>>to continue with the
installation.

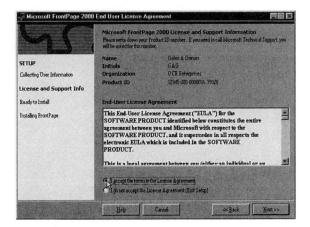

FIGURE 2.3   You must accept the license agreement to install
FrontPage.

5. At the next screen, select the Install Now icon (at the top of the
   screen) to begin installing FrontPage 2000 into C:\Program
   Files\Microsoft Office\, or D:\Program Files\Microsoft Office if
   your programs are installed on your D drive (see Figure 2.4).

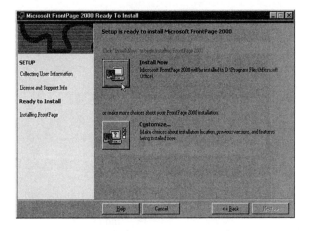

FIGURE 2.4   You can decide during setup where you want
FrontPage installed on your PC.

If you want to install FrontPage into a different folder, select the Customize icon and then enter the name of the folder where you want to install FrontPage. Depending on the speed of your PC, the installation should take approximately 10–20 minutes.

6. When the installation is complete, FrontPage will indicate that and prompt you to select OK to continue. You will then be prompted to restart your PC to complete FrontPage's configuration (see Figure 2.5). Go ahead and select Yes to restart (reboot) your PC.

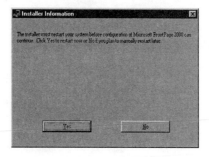

FIGURE 2.5   After installing FrontPage, you need to restart your PC before you can run the program.

If you install FrontPage from the Office 2000 CD-ROM you need to perform a custom installation and select FrontPage to be installed. Here is what you need to do:

1. Insert your FrontPage CD-ROM in your CD-ROM drive.

2. If you do not have the Autorun CD feature turned on then from the Start menu, select Run and type **X:\SETUP**, where *X:* is the drive letter of your CD-ROM drive. In a few seconds, you will see the Maintenance Mode opening screen (see Figure 2.5a).

3. Select Add or Remove Features.

4. Highlight Microsoft FrontPage for Windows (see Figure 2.5b).

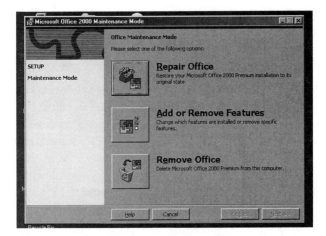

FIGURE 2.5A   Office 2000 Maintenance Mode opening screen.

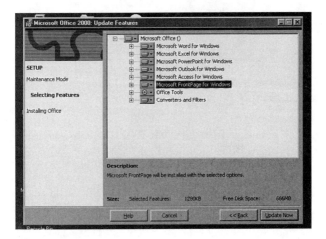

FIGURE 2.5B   Selecting.

5. Select the Update Now button to begin installing FrontPage. The installation procedure begins and in a few minutes the maintenance mode program will indicate that FrontPage was installed.

RUNNING FRONTPAGE FOR THE FIRST TIME

After the installation is completed and your computer has been restarted, you should start FrontPage to make sure the installation went okay, and so you can start becoming familiar with the program.

To start FrontPage for the first time, do the following:

1. Select Programs from the Start menu.

2. Select the Microsoft FrontPage icon to start the program (see Figure 2.6). The program begins in a few seconds.

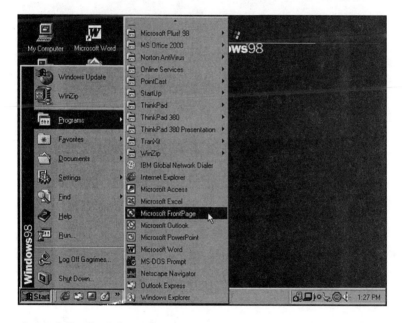

FIGURE 2.6   The Microsoft FrontPage icon you use to start FrontPage.

Shortcut   You can save yourself a little time and effort in starting FrontPage by creating a shortcut on your desktop or your Quick Launch toolbar if you are using Windows 98 and IE4.

3. In a few seconds, you will see the opening screen and then the FrontPage main interface (see Figure 2.7).

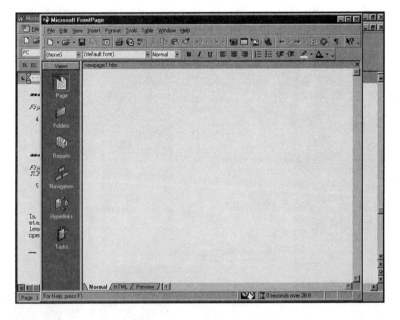

FIGURE 2.7   The main FrontPage 2000 user interface.

4. The first time you start FrontPage, it will take a few minutes to acquire your PC's hostname and TCP/IP address. You may also be prompted as to whether you want to set FrontPage as your default HTML editor. This is information it will need later when you use FrontPage to publish your Web to the Internet (see Figure 2.8).

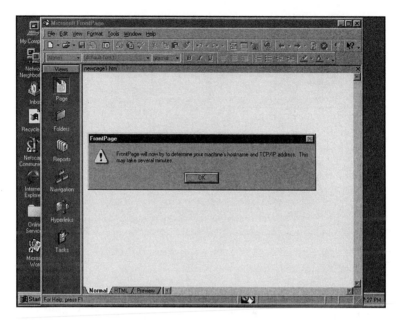

FIGURE 2.8   FrontPage attempts to acquire your PC's hostname and TCP/IP address the first time you start the program.

5. Take a few minutes to look over the user interface to start getting familiar with it. Don't worry about developing a detailed familiarity with the interface now. That will come in the next lesson.

In this lesson, you learned how to install FrontPage on your PC and had some time to become familiar with the main user interface. In the next lesson, you start developing a more detailed familiarity with the operation of the FrontPage editor.

LESSON 3

GETTING FAMILIAR WITH THE FRONTPAGE EDITOR

In this lesson, you begin learning the basic operation of the FrontPage editor.

FRONTPAGE BASICS

The FrontPage editor is probably the most used portion of the entire application. For this reason, you will spend a lot of time learning about it.

Figure 3.1 shows the basic user interface that you see when working in FrontPage.

On the left edge of the screen is the Views Bar. This bar allows you to quickly change not only different views of your Web page but also different functions, such as the Navigation view for creating navigation bars and the Tasks view for adding tasks to your Web. Don't worry about these now. You will learn about these functions in later lessons.

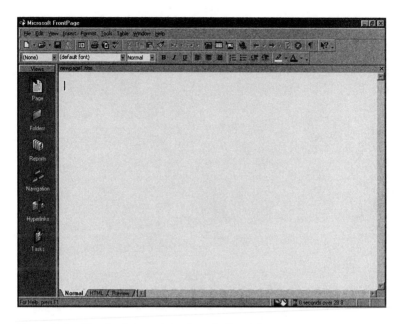

FIGURE 3.1   The basic user interface in FrontPage.

Because you will be spending most of your time using the FrontPage editor, you might find it convenient to remove the Views Bar to allow more
room for your pages to display. To hide the Views Bar

1. Select the View menu.

2. Remove the check mark in front of the Views Bar selection (see
   Figure 3.2), and the Views Bar disappears.

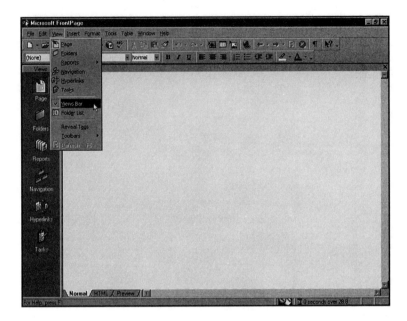

FIGURE 3.2   Removing the Views Bar from the main FrontPage interface.

Notice that even with the Views Bar hidden, you can still access the other views of your Web from the View menu.

Most of the commonly used functions in FrontPage can be accessed from one of the nine standard toolbars. By default the Standard and Formatting toolbars are displayed. But, depending on which functions you tend to use most often, you may want to add additional toolbars to your main interface. Figure 3.3 shows the Standard and Formatting toolbars displayed, and Figure 3.4 shows all nine toolbars displayed.

FIGURE 3.3   FrontPage's main interface with just the Standard and Formatting toolbars displayed.

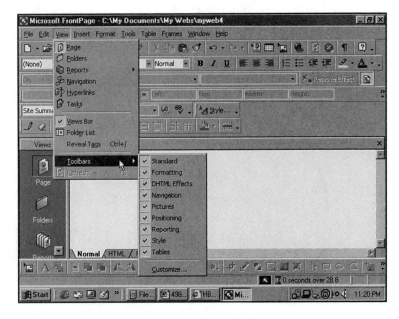

FIGURE 3.4   FrontPage's main interface with all nine toolbars displayed.

HOW TO CREATE A WEB

As mentioned previously, when you create a series of pages for a Web site, FrontPage allows you to group them together as a unit called a Web. While you can still use FrontPage to create and edit individual pages without creating a Web, you are highly encouraged to create a Web to tie your pages together into a cohesive unit for the following reasons:

- FrontPage has several built-in functions to check the validity of your pages and their links.

- FrontPage is designed to allow you to publish your Web to a Web server as a single unit.

- When you create a Web, you can use FrontPage's automatic Navigation tool to create navigation bars for your Web, making it easier for viewers to find their way through your site.

- Keeping your pages in a Web will allows you to use FrontPage's built-in Folders function to organize your files.

- Keeping your pages in a Web allows you to use the FrontPage Reports function to easily check the status of your Web.

Each time you create a new Web, FrontPage creates a new folder using the name of the Web as the name of the folder. Then, any files you create and add to your Web are stored in this folder or subfolders that are created as they are needed.

If this sounds a bit confusing now, don't worry. By the time you complete this lesson this will be a lot clearer.

Create your first Web and you will see. To create a Web

1. From the File menu, select New, Web to open the New Web dialog box (see Figure 3.5).

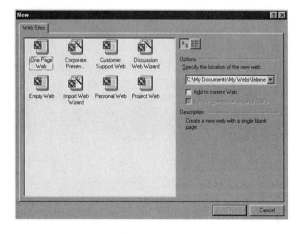

FIGURE 3.5   The New dialog box used to create new Webs.

2. Select the type of Web you want to create from the choice of Web templates. Until you learn more about Web templates in Lesson 4, "Getting Started Using FrontPage Templates," go ahead and select One Page Web.

3. Select the location of the Web folder and a name for your Web.

4. Select OK. If the folder doesn't exist you will be prompted to create the folder. Select Yes to create the folder and Web. In a few seconds, your Web and its corresponding folder are created (see Figure 3.6).

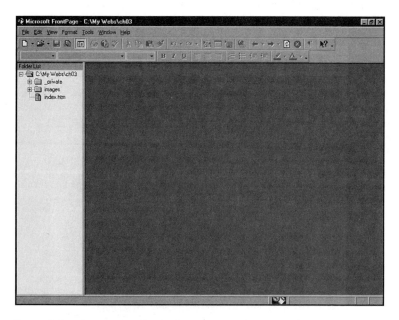

FIGURE 3.6   FrontPage displaying your newly created Web.

How to Create an HTML File

You've learned how to create your Web, now you need to learn how to create pages in your Web. A Web can contain any number of pages.

To add a new page to your Web, do the following:

1. From the File menu, select New, Page to open the New page dialog box (see Figure 3.7).

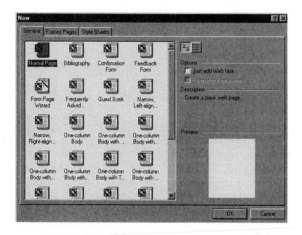

FIGURE 3.7   FrontPage's New dialog box for creating new pages.

2. The New page dialog box displays the various Web page templates available in FrontPage. You learn about using templates in Lesson 4, "Getting Started Using FrontPage Templates." For now, just select Normal Page and select OK. In a few seconds your new blank page appears.

When you create new pages, they will have the default filenames **newpage1.htm**, **newpage2.htm**, and so on. You should save your pages with different, more descriptive filenames to make them easier to identify.

In this lesson, you learned a few things about FrontPage basics, how to create Webs, and how to add pages to your Web. In the next lesson, you learn about using Web and page templates.

LESSON 4

GETTING STARTED USING FRONTPAGE TEMPLATES

In this lesson, you learn how to use FrontPage templates for creating Webs and Web pages.

WHAT ARE TEMPLATES?

Templates are preformed structures you use to build various types of Webs and Web pages. While templates can be preformed structures, they are also "empty" preformed structures, meaning that templates are only the skeletons or the frameworks you use to form the final product.

If you're having trouble with the concept of a template, think of it this way. Imagine the framework of a house being built. The framework is composed of the wooden studs that form the basic shape of the walls and rooms. Working from the framework, you can make the interior and exterior look any way you like. You can use brick or siding on the exterior and plaster walls or paneling on the interior. The point is, the framework is just the structure you build on, which allows you to construct the final product to look any way you want.

Templates work the same way in FrontPage. They are merely the structures on which you build.

TYPES OF TEMPLATES AVAILABLE WITH FRONTPAGE

As you saw briefly in the last lesson, there are two types of templates you can use in FrontPage—Web templates and page templates.

WEB TEMPLATES

FrontPage offers you a choice of eight different Web templates from which to choose when you create a new Web (see Figure 4.1).

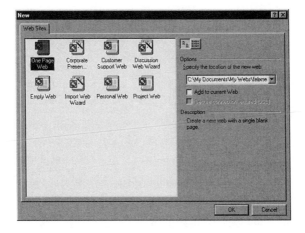

FIGURE **4.1**   FrontPage's choice of Web templates.

The Web templates included in FrontPage are empty structures you can use to construct certain types of Web sites. In addition to the empty Web structures, FrontPage also includes wizards, which are automated templates you can use to create more sophisticated Web structures.

The following is a breakdown of the Web templates and wizards included in FrontPage:

- *Corporate Presence Wizard*—This wizard guides you through the steps of creating a Web presence for your business.

- *Customer Support Web*—This is a Web template you can use to create a customer support Web site; especially good for software companies looking to create Web-based support sites.

- *Discussion Web Wizard*—This wizard guides you through creating a Web-based newsgroup type discussion site.

- *Import Web Wizard*—This wizard allows you to create a type of Web-based textual archive from files on your local computer. You can also use this wizard to import an existing Web site into a FrontPage Web.

- *Project Web*—Create a Web based on a specific project including the project's schedule, status, project numbers, archives, and discussions.

- *Personal Web*—You can use this Web template to create your own personal Web site that reflects your activities and interests.

- *One Page Web*—This is a simple Web template containing one blank Web page.

- *Empty Web*—This is an even simpler Web template that contains no pages.

USING A WEB WIZARD TEMPLATE

The simpler Web templates, those that do not incorporate a wizard, are a snap to operate. To use a simple template to create a Web, do the following:

1. From the File menu, select New, Web to open the New Web Sites template dialog box.

2. Select the type of Web template you want to use, such as Customer Support Web (see Figure 4.2).

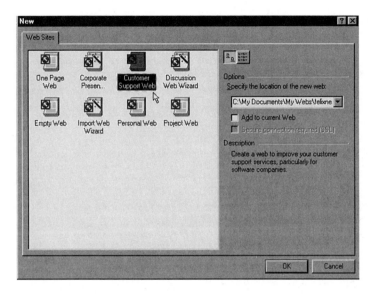

FIGURE 4.2   Selecting a Web template in FrontPage.

3. Select the directory or folder where you want to create the Web and select OK.

4. You will be prompted to create the directory if it does not already exist. Answer Yes, and FrontPage begins creating the template.

5. In a few seconds your template is created (see Figure 4.3).

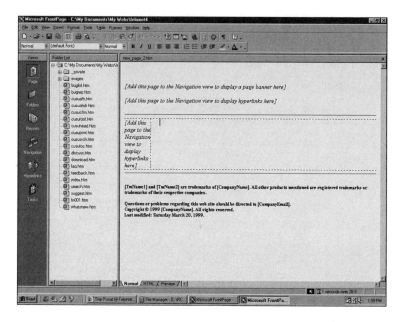

FIGURE 4.3   The new Web created by FrontPage.

In all of the Web templates except Empty Web, FrontPage will add one or more page templates to the Web.

USING PAGE TEMPLATES TO CREATE DIFFERENT TYPES OF WEB PAGES

Just like Web templates, page templates are also empty structures you can use to create the pages in your Web site. And, just as with Web templates, you can create as many pages as you need or want by using page templates.

While FrontPage only offers you a choice of eight different Web templates, it offers you a choice of 36 different page templates. Figure 4.4 shows you most of the page templates from which you can choose.

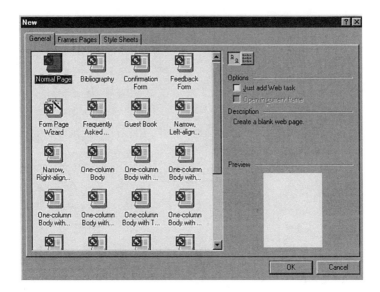

FIGURE 4.4   Some of the page templates you can choose from in FrontPage.

Unlike Web templates, FrontPage displays a simple schematic of each page template before you actually create it.

To create a page using a page template, do the following:

1. From the File menu, select New, Page to open the New page template dialog box.

2. Select the type of page template you want to use such as Narrow, Left-aligned Body (see Figure 4.5).

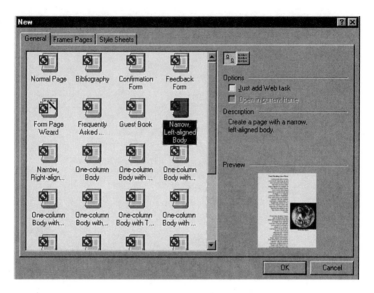

FIGURE 4.5   Selecting the Narrow, Left-aligned Body page template in FrontPage.

The page template you select displays a schematic in the Preview window.

3. Select OK and in a few seconds your new page is created from the template you selected (see Figure 4.6).

You will notice, as you begin to experiment and use the Web templates that include pages, that FrontPage creates those pages by using some of the same page templates from which you just chose.

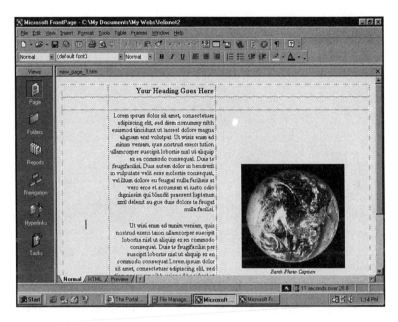

FIGURE 4.6   Your new page, created from a FrontPage template.

In this lesson, you learned how to create Webs and Web pages by using templates in FrontPage. In the next lesson, you learn how to begin adding text to your pages.

LESSON 5

WORKING WITH TEXT

In this lesson, you learn how to enter text onto your Web pages.

TEXT BASICS

Now that you've covered most of the basics in terms of getting FrontPage installed and learning how to create Webs and pages, it's time to start learning how to add content to your pages.

First and foremost, you will learn how to add text to your pages. If you've spent much time surfing the Web, you may have noticed that what you see on most Web sites is text. This is understandable, because most sites are set up to convey some type of information, and text is still one of the most efficient means to do so.

FrontPage doesn't only allow you enter basic text on your pages. It also gives you a tremendous amount freedom to "dress up" your text. Besides putting basic letters on the page with FrontPage you can

- Adjust the size of your text

- Adjust the position of your text as either subscript or superscript

- Give your text attributes such as **bold**, *italic*, or <u>underline</u>, or any combination of these attributes

- Center your text on the screen

- Add color or other effects such as blinking to your text
- Change the font that is displayed onscreen

This is just a small sampling of some of the ways you can modify your text. As you will see as you begin to work more with FrontPage a large portion of what you will be entering on your Web pages is text, and FrontPage offers you a tremendous amount of flexibility in how you do that.

PUTTING TEXT ON THE PAGE

Putting text on the your pages in FrontPage is as simple as putting text on a page in your word processing program—all you do is type. And just like with your word processing program, when you reach the end of a line, your text wraps automatically to the next line.

Begin by typing a familiar paragraph:

1. If you don't already have a blank page on your screen, create a new page by selecting File, New, Page. Then select Normal Page from the New Page dialog box and select OK to open your page.

2. At the cursor, type the following:

   The Gettysburg Address

3. Press the Enter key and the continue typing the following text. Don't press the Enter key when you reach the end of the line, just keep typing and let the text wrap to the next line.

   Four score and seven years ago our fathers brought forth on this continent a new nation, conceived in liberty and dedicated to the proposition that all men are created equal.

4. Press the Enter key when you finish typing this paragraph. Your text should look similar to what you see in Figure 5.1.

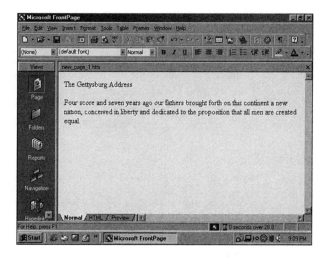

FIGURE 5.1   Sample text entered on a blank page.

Just like with any other Windows-based text-processing program, to add
an attribute to your text, you need to highlight the text you want to
change.

Begin by changing the size of the text, one of the most common attributes
you'll see on Web pages. To change the size of your text, do the
following:

1. Highlight the text "The Gettysburg Address."

2. On the Format menu, select Font to open the Font formatting
   dialog box. In the Size section, scroll down to the selection 7 (36
   pt). Select OK. Your text should now look like the text shown in
   Figure 5.2.

Shortcut Menu   You don't have to use the Format
menu to access the Font formatting dialog box. You
can also right-click to open a shortcut menu, and
select Font Properties to open the Font formatting
dialog box.

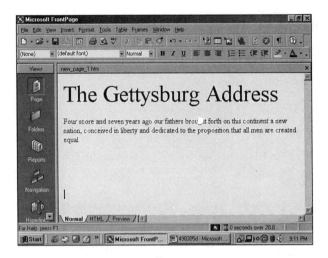

FIGURE 5.2   Formatted text showing a change in size.

FrontPage gives you a fair amount of latitude in setting the size of your text. Figure 5.3 shows you the range you have in setting text size, from 8 to 36 points.

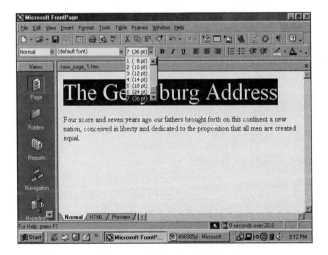

FIGURE 5.3   You can adjust the size of your text from 8 to 36 points.

ADDING COLOR AND ATTRIBUTES

Ok, now add some attributes to your text to make it a bit more dramatic.
Start by changing the color of the title. You're still working with the
Gettysburg Address paragraph.

To change the color of your text

1. Highlight the text "The Gettysburg Address."

2. From the Format menu, select Font to open the Font dialog box
   (see Figure 5.4).

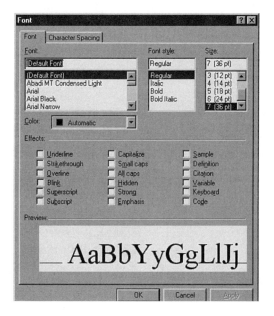

FIGURE 5.4   The Font formatting dialog box.

3. Select the Color dropbox to open the Color palette.

4. Select Red and select OK to close the Font formatting dialog
   box. The paragraph title should now be set to red.

In addition to changing the color of your text, you can also set your text
to be bold, italic, or underlined.

To add bold to your text

1. Highlight the words "Four score and seven years ago."

2. Select the Bold icon (it's a bold B) on the toolbar. The text you highlighted should now be bold.

To add italics to your text

1. Highlight the words "on this continent."

2. Select the Italics icon (it's an italicized I) on the toolbar. The text you highlighted should now be italicized.

To underline your text

1. Highlight the word "liberty."

2. Select the Underline icon (it's an underlined U) on the toolbar. The text you highlighted should now be underlined.

3. Your paragraph should now look like the one in Figure 5.5.

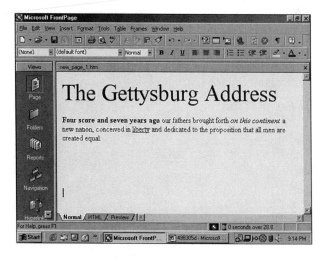

FIGURE 5.5 Your text after applying a few attributes.

FONT STYLES AND EFFECTS

FrontPage still has a few tricks up its sleeve to offer when you want to make changes to your text.

The following are a few examples:

1. Highlight the word "fathers."

2. From the Format menu, select Font to open the Font formatting dialog box.

3. In the Effects section, you can see the various effects FrontPage allows you to use on your text. The Preview window allows you to see how each change affects your text. Notice the lines on either side of the text in the Preview window. These lines allow you to see the relative position of your text for effects that change the vertical positioning of your text, such as subscript and superscript.

4. Select Small Caps and Superscript. Select OK to close the dialog box and see the changes you just made to your text (see Figure 5.6).

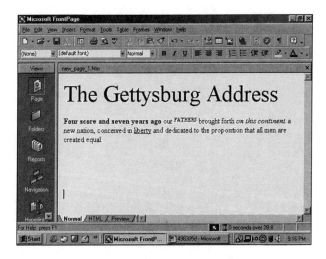

FIGURE 5.6   Using additional formatting effects on your text.

Changing character spacing is another effect you can use to accent your text. The Character Spacing set of effects allows you to adjust the spacing between characters and to adjust their vertical positioning (either above or below the line) relative to the rest of the text on the line.

Take a look at some of the things you can do with character spacing:

1. Highlight the text "on this continent."

2. Open the Font formatting dialog box.

3. Select the Character Spacing tab to open the Character Spacing sheet (see Figure 5.7).

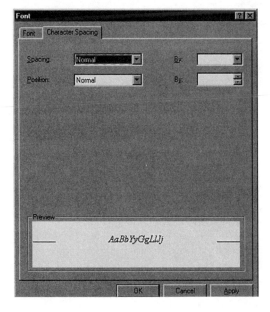

FIGURE 5.7 The Character Spacing tab in the Font formatting dialog box.

4. In the Spacing dropbox, select Expanded. In the By dropbox next to Spacing, select 10.

5. In the Position dropbox, select Raised. In the By dropbox next to Position, enter 5.

6. Select OK to save your character spacing changes and view your text (see Figure 5.8).

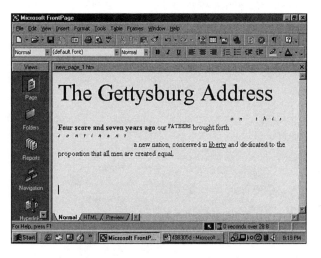

FIGURE 5.8   Your sample text showing more changes in spacing.

As you can see, character spacing effects offer you a lot of freedom in adjusting the spacing and positioning of your text.

In this lesson, you learned how to enter text on your Web pages and how to initiate some of the basic attribute and effects changes. In the next lesson, you learn how to use tables on your pages.

LESSON 6
WORKING WITH TABLES

In this lesson, you learn how to create and use tables on your Web pages.

UNDERSTANDING TABLES

Mastering the use of tables on your Web pages allows you an incredible amount of control for positioning both text and images.

Tables are rectangular grid structures you can create on your pages to contain text or images. Figure 6.1 displays some examples of tables.

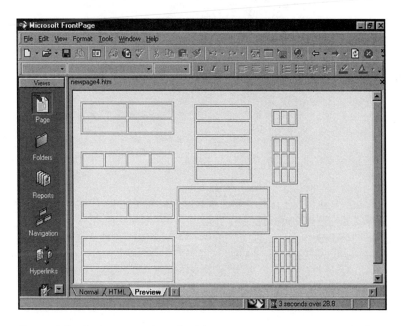

FIGURE 6.1   Some examples of tables you can create on your Web pages.

As you will soon see, tables can take on a variety of shapes and sizes, can be accented with color, and can be invisible depending on how you set their properties.

The rectangular grids composing the structure of a table are called cells. As with other, similar gridwork structures, a horizontal grouping of cells is called a row and a vertical grouping of cells is called a column.

CREATING TABLES

The easiest way to learn about tables is to create and use them. To create a table

1. Create a new, blank page.

2. From the Table menu, select Insert and then Table to open the Insert Table dialog box (see Figure 6.2).

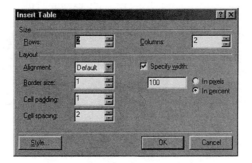

FIGURE 6.2   The Insert Table dialog box.

3. The default size for a new table is two rows by two columns for a total of four cells. Go ahead for now and accept this default size. Also accept the default values for Layout and Width. You will learn how to change these values later. Select OK, and your table is created on the page (see Figure 6.3).

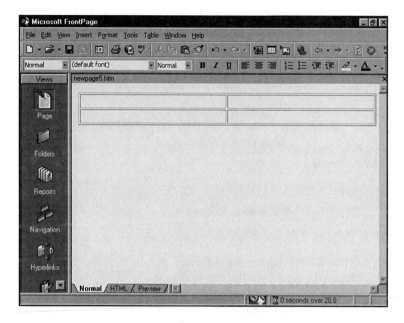

FIGURE 6.3   A table with the default size of two rows by two columns.

UNDERSTANDING TABLE SIZES

One of the first things you need to learn about tables is how they are sized. You may have noticed that table widths are set either as a percentage or in *pixels*.

Pixels   Picture elements, or pixels, are the smallest units used together to display information on your monitor. You most often hear the term used to describe the resolution of your video display. For example, common resolutions are 640×480 or 800×600. These refer to the number of pixels displayed on your screen (horizontal×vertical).

If you accepted the default width for the table you created earlier, your table was set to 100 percent of the display area. So, regardless of the resolution of the monitor displaying the page, the table will fill 100 percent of the screen's width. When you select the width of your table as a percentage, it is a relative width—relative to the width of your display area.

On the other hand, if you select the width of your table in terms of pixels, you set an absolute width. For example, if you create a table with a width of 500 pixels, that table will always be 500 pixels, regardless of the display resolution.

To change the width of your table

1. Place you cursor inside the table.

2. From the Table menu, choose Select, Table.

3. From the Table menu, select Properties, Table to open the Table Properties dialog box (see Figure 6.4).

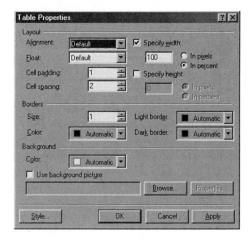

FIGURE 6.4   The Table Properties dialog box.

4. In the Specify Width section, select the In Pixels radio button and set the value to **400**.

5. Select OK and your table is resized.

Table Height   You can also adjust the height of your tables from the Table Properties dialog box even though most Web page designers don't consider table height to be as a important as table width. Table height usually adjusts automatically, depending on what's inside the table or the individual cells. If you decide to change the height of your table, you can only make absolute adjustments in pixels. Just select the Specify Height check box and then enter the number of pixels you want for the height.

WORKING WITH TABLE LAYOUT

The best way to point out table layout features is to show them to you in a somewhat exaggerated manner. Continue working with the table you created earlier in this lesson, and set the layout features to values a lot higher than you might normally set them. Exaggerating the setting will help illustrate their function.

Start with border size. Border size refers to the size of the outside border of the table measured in pixels.

To change the border size on your table

1. Select the table you created earlier.

2. From the Table menu, select Properties, Table to open the Table Properties dialog box.

3. In the Borders section, change Border Size to **20**.

4. Select OK to initiate the change in border size and to view the change you just made (see Figure 6.5).

Invisible Borders   There's also another cool trick you can do with your borders setting. Set border size to 0, and your border becomes invisible when displayed by a Web browser. This is useful if you want to use tables to lay out text and graphics.

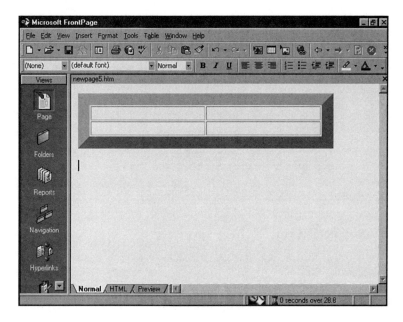

FIGURE 6.5   Table with a border size set to 20.

Cell padding is another layout feature you can adjust. Cell padding refers to the amount of space between the table cell's contents and the inner edges of the cells. Cell padding is also measured in pixels.

To change cell padding

1. Select the table you created earlier.

2. From the Table menu, select Properties, Table to open the Table Properties dialog box.

3. In the Layout section, change Cell Padding to 20.

4. Select OK to initiate the change in cell padding and to view the change you just made (see Figure 6.6).

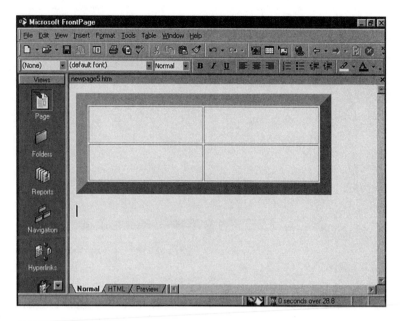

FIGURE 6.6   Table with cell padding set to 20.

Cell spacing is another layout feature you can use to alter the appearance of your tables. Cell spacing refers to the amount of space between the individual cells in a table. Cell spacing is also measured in pixels.

To change cell spacing

1. Select the table you created earlier.

2. From the Table menu, select Properties, Table to open the Table Properties dialog box.

3. In the Layout section, change Cell Spacing to 20.

4. Select OK to initiate the change in cell spacing and to view the change you just made (see Figure 6.7).

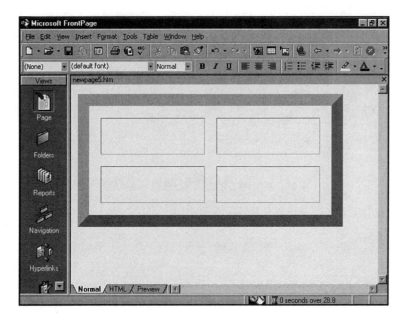

FIGURE 6.7   Table with cell spacing set to 20.

WORKING WITH TABLE COLORS

In addition to setting the size of your table's borders, you can set the colors of your borders and the background of your table.

You can set just the border, or you can create a 3-dimensional effect by setting what are called light borders and dark borders.

To set the border color of your table

1. Select the table you created earlier.

2. From the Table menu, select Properties, Table to open the Table Properties dialog box.

3. In the Border section, select the dropbox for Color to open the Border Color palette.

4. Select Red for the color of your table's border.

5. Select OK to initiate the change in color and to view the change you just made.

You can also set border colors to simulate a type of 3-dimensional effect with your borders. The 3-dimensional effect is achieved by using light and dark border colors. While you may need to experiment with various color combinations to achieve the best results, here is a brief example to help illustrate the point.

To set 3-dimensional colors for your borders

1. Select the table you created earlier.

2. From the Table menu, select Properties, Table to open the Table Properties dialog box.

3. In the Border section, select the dropbox for Light Border to open the Light Border Color palette.

4. Select Red for the color of your table's light border.

5. In the Border Colors section, select the dropbox for Dark Border to open the Dark Border Color palette.

6. Select Maroon for the color of your table's dark border.

7. Select OK to initiate the change in color and to view the change you just made (see Figure 6.8).

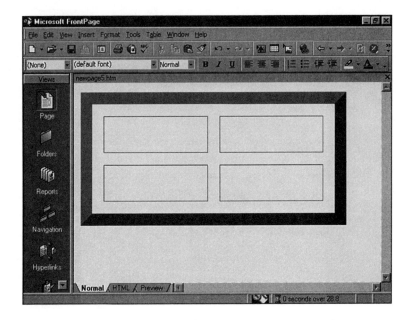

FIGURE 6.8   A table with both light and dark border colors set to simulate a 3D effect.

In this lesson, you learned how to create tables and began to make some modifications in how your tables look by also changing their size and color. In the next lesson, you learn more about modifying your tables.

LESSON 7
DOING MORE WITH TABLES

In this lesson, you learn more about working with the tables you create for your Web pages.

MANIPULATING THE CELLS IN A TABLE

After you created your first table, you may have thought long and hard about how much thought you would need to put into creating future tables. The answer is none! Even though you have to specify the number of rows and columns in your table when you create it, you are not locked into that configuration of cells. You can add or remove cells from your table at any time. You can also split one cell into two or more cells, and you can merge two or more cells into one.

ADDING CELLS

When you want to add to your table, FrontPage gives you the option of adding a single cell or one or more rows or columns.

To add a new row to your table

1. Just as you did back in Lesson 6, "Working with Tables," create a simple table with the default values of two rows and two columns.

2. Select one of the cells in the table by clicking in the cell you want to select.

3. From the Table menu, select Insert, Rows or Columns to open the Insert Rows or Columns dialog box (see Figure 7.1).

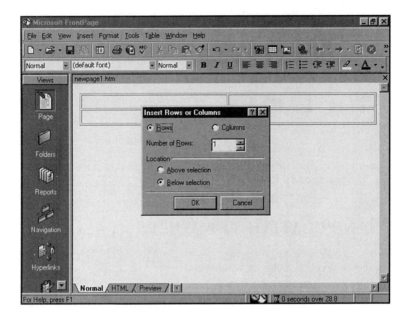

FIGURE 7.1   The Insert Rows or Columns dialog box.

4. Select the Rows radio button to insert one or more rows to your table.

5. Select the number of rows you want to insert in your table. You can add anywhere from 1–1000 rows.

6. Under Location, select whether you want to add your new row(s) above or below the cell where your cursor is currently situated.

7. Select OK to complete the insert and close the dialog box (see Figure 7.2).

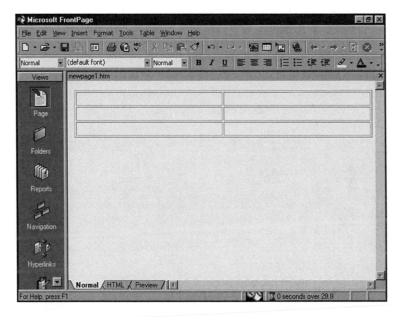

Figure 7.2   Your table with its newly added cells.

Adding Tables Within Tables   In addition to being able to add cells, rows, or columns to your table, FrontPage also allows you to add a new table inside another table. You simply select the cell you want to put the table into and follow the previous instructions for creating a table.

SPLITTING CELLS

Sometimes, instead of adding an additional cell to your table, you decide
instead that it would be better to simply split one cell into two or more
cells. Figure 7.3 shows you a before and after example. The top row of
the table shows you two cells in the row. The second and third rows show
the cells in the left column split into two cells.

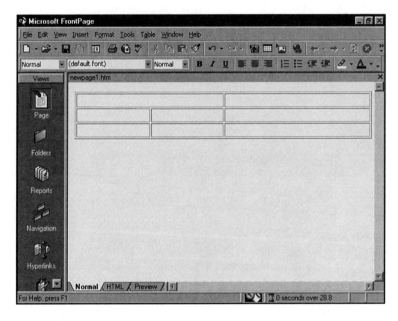

FIGURE 7.3   An example of a table with split cells.

To split a cell into two or more cells

1. Select one of the cells in the table you want to split by clicking
    in that cell.

2. From the Table menu, select Split Cells to open the Split Cells
    dialog box (see Figure 7.4).

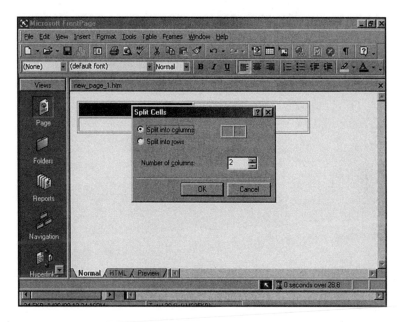

FIGURE 7.4   The Split Cells dialog box.

3. Select whether you want to Split into Columns or Split into
   Rows.

4. Select the number of columns or rows you want to split the cell
   into. The default is 2; the maximum is 100.

5. Select OK to close the dialog box and initiate the split (see
   Figure 7.5).

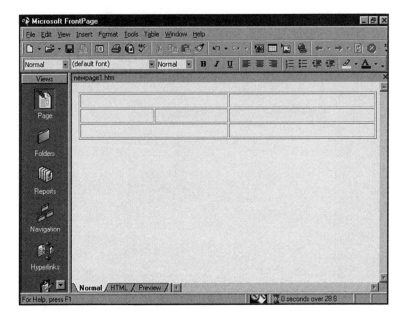

FIGURE 7.5   A table with a cell split into 2 cells.

MERGING CELLS

It stands to reason that if you can split your cells you can also reverse the process and merge them.

To merge two or more cells

1. Select the first cell you want to include in your merge and place the cursor in that cell.

2. Hold down the Shift key and select the adjacent cell you want to merge with the previously selected cell. The two cells you have chosen should be highlighted (see Figure 7.6).

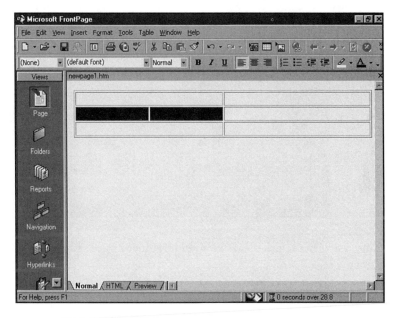

FIGURE 7.6 The two highlighted cells you want to merge.

3. From the Table menu, select Merge Cells and the cells you selected are merged into one (see Figure 7.7).

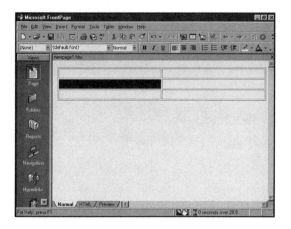

FIGURE 7.7   The selected cells merged into one.

DELETING CELLS

Deleting cells from your table is just as easy as adding cells.

To delete one or more cells from your table

1. Decide whether you want to delete a cell, a row, or a column in your table.

2. Select by clicking in a cell of the cell, row, or column you want to delete.

3. From the Table menu, choose Select, Cell (or Row or Column, depending on what you intend to delete).

4. With the portion of the table selected that you want to delete, again open the Table menu and select Delete Cells. Your selection is deleted.

DISTRIBUTING ROWS AND COLUMNS EVENLY

Sometimes you can get carried away merging and splitting cells in a table or adding and deleting cells, and you wind up with an uneven table with rows and columns of varying sizes. FrontPage includes commands to distribute your rows or columns evenly to remedy this problem. For example, if you have a table that looks like the one in Figure 7.8 you can redistribute the cells in the second row to make them all even.

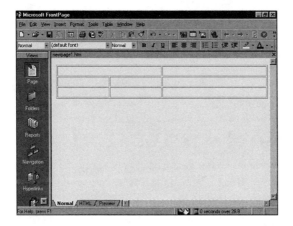

FIGURE 7.8   Redistributing the cells in the second row to make them all even.

To redistribute an uneven row in a table

1. Select the table containing the rows or columns you want to redistribute evenly.

2. From the Table menu, select Distribute Rows (or Columns) Evenly, and your rows or columns (whichever you selected) are redistributed into a more even pattern.

Granted, what's even and what's not may sometimes be in the eyes of the beholder. But if you do redistribute your table's rows or columns and don't think the distribution is exactly what you want, you can always select the Undo command from the Edit menu and your table will revert to the way it was before you did your redistribution.

In this lesson, you learned a few more tips about working with tables. These basics will come in handy very shortly when you learn how to use your tables to control the layout of your Web pages. But, before you get to that stage in your understanding of FrontPage, there are still a few more basic lessons you need to learn first. In the next lesson, you learn how to create lists.

Lesson 8

Creating Lists

In this lesson, you learn how to use FrontPage to create lists on your Web pages.

Types of Lists You Can Create

The text you enter on your Web pages is not always best displayed in sentence or paragraph form. Sometimes you need to create lists of items.

FrontPage offers you a choice of creating either bulleted lists (see Figure 8.1) or numbered lists (see Figure 8.2).

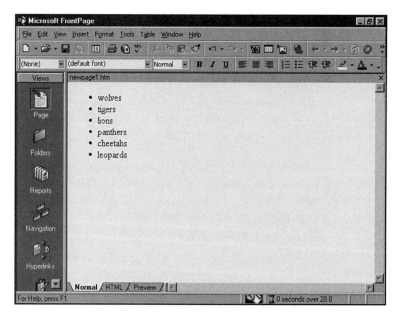

FIGURE 8.1   An example of a bulleted list.

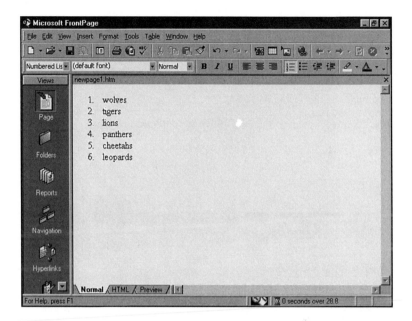

FIGURE 8.2   An example of a numbered list.

Lists on Web pages are used in pretty much the same way that lists are used anywhere else—to group together similar items or to show a progression of some type.

CREATING YOUR LISTS

When you decide you want to place a list on one of your Web pages FrontPage gives you the option of three different types of lists:

- A numbered list
- A bulleted list
- An image bulleted list

Let's create one of each type so you can see the differences in all three types.

CREATING A NUMBERED LIST

Numbered lists are typically used when you want to show some type of progression such as the steps required to perform a certain task. The steps in this book detailing how to perform various operations in FrontPage are examples of numbered lists.

Here's how to create a numbered list in FrontPage:

1. Create a list showing steps to perform a task or some sort of progression. For example, how to hang a picture on a wall. See the steps listed in Figure 8.3.

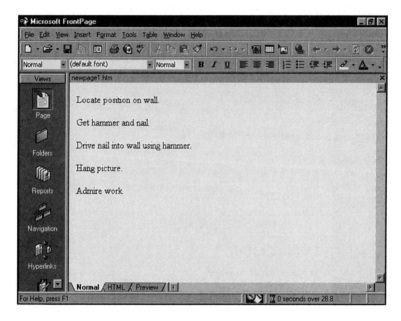

FIGURE 8.3   An example set of steps to be turned into a numbered list.

2. Highlight all of the text that will comprise your list.

3. From the Format menu, select Bullets and Numbering to open the Bullets and Numbering dialog box (see Figure 8.4).

FIGURE 8.4   The Bullets and Numbering dialog box.

4. Select the Numbers tab to open the Numbers sheet (see Figure 8.5).

FIGURE 8.5   The Numbers sheet in the Bullets and Numbering dialog box.

5. Select the type of numbering you want to use to format your list.

6. If you want to start your numbered list with a value other than 1 (or A) from the Start At box select and increment your starting value.

7. Select OK to close the dialog box and create your list (see Figure 8.6).

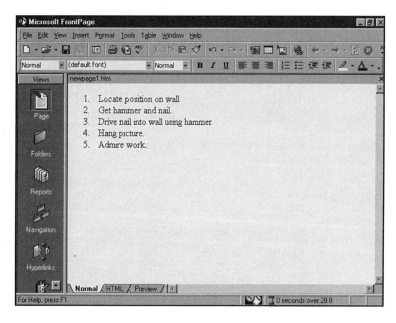

FIGURE 8.6   Your newly created numbered list.

CREATING BULLETED LISTS

Bulleted lists are sometimes also referred to as "un-ordered" or "un-numbered" lists. While numbered lists are generally used to illustrate some sort of progression, un-numbered lists are typically used just to show some type of grouping of items. Regardless of how or why you use un-numbered lists, what's important for now is simply learning how to create them.

FrontPage allows you to create two types of bulleted or "un-numbered" lists—lists created using plain bullets and lists created using image bullets.

Lists created using plain bullets are probably already familiar to you. FrontPage also allows you to create lists using image files. FrontPage includes several small image files you can use for bullets, or you can use image files of your own choosing.

 If you choose your own image files to use as bullets, make sure you choose small image files. Try to use images in the shapes of balls, diamonds, squares, or other small images.

First, let's create a bulleted list:

1. Create a list of items.

2. Highlight all of the text that will comprise your list.

3. From the Format menu, select Bullets and Numbering to open the Bullets and Numbering dialog box.

4. Select the Plain Bullets tab to open the Plain Bullets sheet.

5. Select the type of bullet you want to use to format your list.

6. Select OK to close the dialog box and create your list (see Figure 8.7).

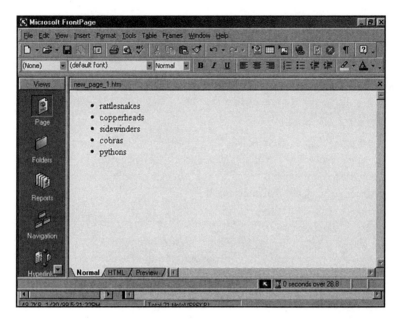

FIGURE 8.7   A sample bulleted list.

Creating a bulleted list with image bullets is just about as easy as creating a list with plain bullets.

To create a list with image bullets

1. Create a list of items.

2. Highlight all of the text that will comprise your list.

3. From the Format menu, select Bullets and Numbering to open the Bullets and Numbering dialog box.

4. Select the Picture Bullets tab to open the Picture Bullets sheet.

5. Select the image you want to use for your image bullets. If you are using a theme you can select a bullet image associated with your page theme. Select the Use picture from Current Theme radio button. If you are not using a theme with your page, you

can select the image you want to use. Select the Specify Picture radio button and then enter the filename for the image file you want to use. If you are not sure of the filename or the location of the file, you can use the Browse button to locate the image file you want to use.

6. Select OK to close the dialog box and create your image file bulleted list (see Figure 8.8).

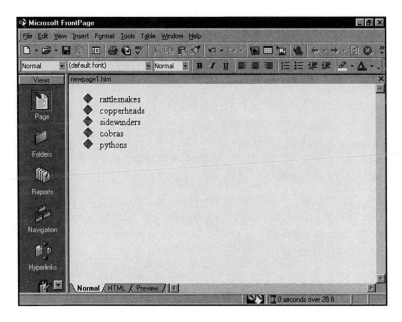

FIGURE 8.8   A bulleted list using image bullets.

In this lesson, you learned how to create lists on your Web pages. You can create both numbered lists and bulleted lists using FrontPage. If you choose to create bulleted lists, FrontPage allows you to create lists using image files as your bullets. In the next lesson, you learn how to use graphics and images in your files.

LESSON 9

WORKING WITH GRAPHICS AND IMAGES

In this lesson, you learn how to add images to your Web pages.

GRAPHICS AND IMAGES BASICS

Back in Lesson 5, "Working with Text," when you leaned how to add text to your pages, you learned that text is the "meat and potatoes" of your Web pages. Well, in this lesson you learn how to add graphics to your pages, what some might refer to as the "gravy."

The term *graphics* usually refers to any visual, non-text element on a Web page. The term *images* usually refers to static graphic files in one of two native Web formats—GIF (Graphics Interchange Format) or JPEG (Joint Photographic Expert Group).

When the World Wide Web was first created, it was a text-only service. It wasn't until someone figured out how to include pictures that interest in the Web exploded. Pictures do more than just help illustrate your text. As the saying goes "…a picture is worth a thousand words," and nowhere is this maxim illustrated better than on the World Wide Web. Pictures add an extra dimension to your text and can be a tremendous help in explaining the information you are trying to convey on your pages.

Regardless of why you are using pictures or images on your pages, the purpose of this lesson is to teach you how to do it.

Before you begin, there are few "rules" or suggestions you need to be aware of when using images, which will help make your pages more enjoyable for others to view.

1. *Use small image files*—Everything you see with your Web browser is downloaded to your PC for display and that includes image files. Larger files take longer to download to the PC of the person viewing your pages, which means it will take longer to display your pages if you populate them with lots of large files.

2. *Keep the number of image files you use per page to a minimum*—Having a lot of image files on a page is just as bad as having a few large image files. No one likes to wait for a Web page to display.

3. *Don't just add an image because you have extra images to add*—Unless you are creating a page that is a photo album, make sure your images contribute something to the content of your page.

One thing you can do to make the creation of your Web pages easier is to create an \IMAGES folder in your Web directory in which to store all of your image files. When you create a Web, an \IMAGES folder is created for you by default in the Web where you should store your image files. If you create a Web in a directory outside of FrontPage, make sure you also create an \IMAGES folder for your image files.

ADDING IMAGES WITH FRONTPAGE

Inserting an image onto your Web page by using FrontPage is as easy as adding text.

To insert an image onto your page

1. Open a new page in your Web in FrontPage.

2. From the Insert menu, select Picture, From File to open the Picture dialog box (see Figure 9.1).

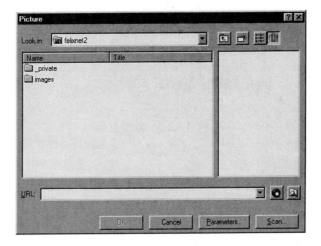

FIGURE 9.1   The Picture dialog box is used for selecting the image you want to insert in your page.

3. Select the image file you want to insert onto your page.

4. Select OK and the image file appears on your page (see Figure 9.2).

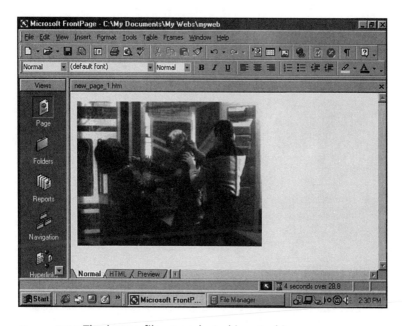

FIGURE 9.2 The image file you selected inserted in your page.

5. From the File menu, select Save to open the Save As dialog box (see Figure 9.3) to make sure your image file is saved with your Web and also saved in your \IMAGES folder.

6. If the folder is not set to your \IMAGES folder, select the Change Folder button, select \IMAGES, and then OK.

7. Select OK to save your image file with your Web.

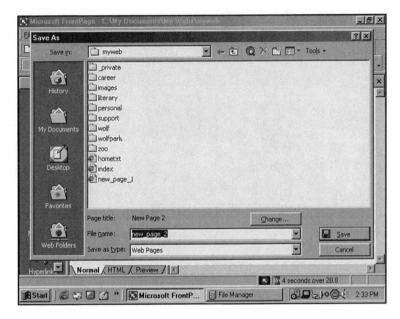

FIGURE 9.3   The Save As dialog box.

MODIFYING YOUR IMAGE FILES

Once you get your image files inserted into your pages, there's still a lot more you can do to control how your image files will be displayed. These display settings include:

- Controlling the dimensions of the image on the page

- Controlling the way text aligns with the image

- Controlling whether the image file is displayed with a border

- Adding a hyperlink to your image file

Keep in mind that just because you can make these changes and modifications to your image files doesn't mean you are required to do so. All of these modifications are optional. They are available for your use if you decide you want to use them.

To modify how your images are displayed

1. Select the image file you want to modify.

2. From the Format menu, select Properties to open the Picture
    Properties dialog box (see Figure 9.4).

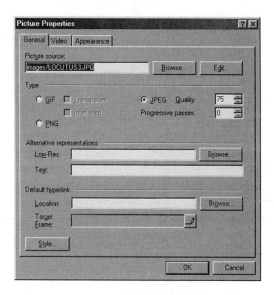

FIGURE 9.4   The Picture Properties dialog box.

3. To add a hyperlink to your image file, enter the URL for the
    hyperlink you want to associate with this image file in the
    Default Hyperlink section of the dialog box. The URL can be to
    another Web site (for example, http://www.felixnet.com) or to
    another file on your site (for example, inventory.htm). You can
    use the Browse button to locate the URL if you cannot remem-
    ber it.

4. To modify the dimensions of the image file, select the
    Appearance tab to open the Appearance sheet (see Figure 9.5).

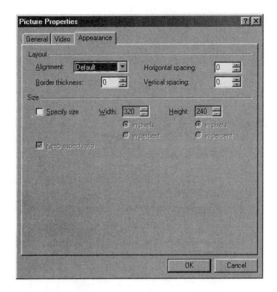

FIGURE 9.5   The Appearance sheet in the Picture Properties
dialog box.

5. Change the width or height value of the image file to change the
display dimensions of the file. You can make your changes in
pixels or as a percentage of the file's original dimensions.

Make sure you leave the Keep Aspect Ratio check box
selected, otherwise your image will be distorted when
it is displayed on your page.

6. Select OK to save your changes and close the Picture Properties
dialog box.

Perhaps the most frequent changes you are likely to make in your image
file settings deal with the layout of the files, especially with regard to how
text flows around your image files. FrontPage allows you to exercise a fair
amount of control when it comes to determining how your text interacts
with your image files.

The following example will help you understand how alignment works when text and image files interact.

To test text alignment

1. Create a new page.

2. Type the following sentence on your page:

   This is an example of how text can be set to wrap around your image files.

3. Place your cursor before the word "This" and insert a sample image. If the size of the image is more than 150 pixels wide, adjust the image size so that it is no wider than 150 pixels. Your page should look similar to Figure 9.6.

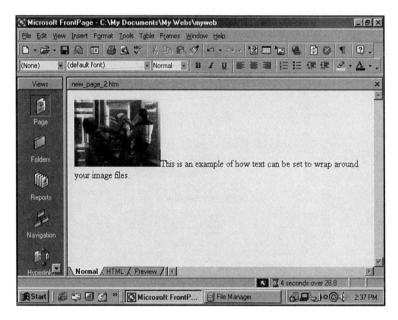

Figure 9.6   Your example text and image for testing alignment.

4. Select the image you inserted and open the Picture Properties dialog box. Select the Appearance tab to open the Appearance sheet.

5. Your image should have Default alignment. To see how changes in the alignment can affect the flow of text next to and around an image, change the type of alignment in the Alignment dropbox and note how the image and text change.

In this lesson, you learned how to insert images into your pages and how to modify their settings to change how they are displayed. In the next lesson, you learn more about how to control the placement of images on your pages.

LESSON 10

CONTROLLING IMAGES IN FRONTPAGE 2000

In this lesson, you learn more about controlling the placement of images on your Web pages.

POSITIONING YOUR GRAPHICS WITH FRONTPAGE

In the preceding lesson, you learned how to insert images into your pages. Now you're going to learn a few tricks on how to position your images. Bear in mind that creating Web pages is still as much an art as it is a science, so while this information can he helpful in some situations, it is by no means absolute.

CONTROLLING YOUR IMAGE FILES USING TABLES

Controlling images, especially if you want to combine the image with text, is a lot easier if you simply remember something you learned back in Lesson 6, "Working with Tables." Using tables can help you control alignment problems you can encounter, especially if you want to position images and text next to each other or one on top of the other.

To show you how tables can help make it easier to control text and images

1. Create a new page.
2. Create a table on the page that is one row by two columns.
3. Insert your image into the cell on the left.

4. Enter your text in the cell on the right.

5. By simply changing the width of the table to 400 pixels, you can produce results similar to what you see in Figure 10.1.

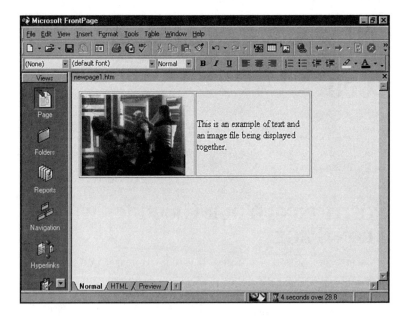

FIGURE 10.1   Text and an image file in a table.

CONTROLLING IMAGE PLACEMENT USING FRONTPAGE TEMPLATES

Another avenue you should pursue to control the placement of images and text was explained back in Lesson 4, "Getting Started Using FrontPage Templates."

Remember templates?

Many of the templates FrontPage includes for your convenience are designed to accommodate a variety of patterns combining text and images (see Figure 10.2).

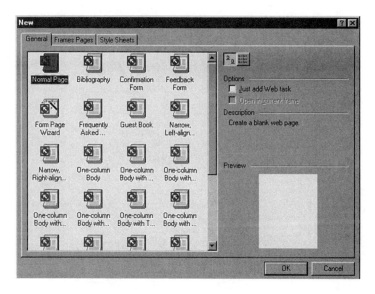

FIGURE **10.2**   FrontPage templates you can use to control placement of text and images.

CREATING THUMBNAILS

Another way you can control images on your pages is by using thumbnails. *Thumbnails* are smaller versions of larger image files and are links to the larger version. While not always thought of as a means of controlling image placement, thumbnails are a convenient means of placing a lot of images on a page and exercising a lot of control over their size.

For an example of thumbnails and how you can use them start your browser, go to http://www.felixnet.com/wolfpark/wp-trip1.htm (see Figure 10.3).

Thumbnails are used when you have several large images you want to present on your Web page but don't want to create an unreasonable delay for viewers or don't want to take up a lot of valuable onscreen real estate.

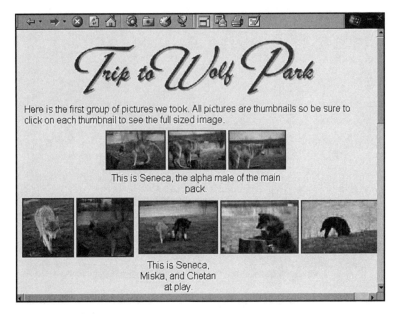

FIGURE 10.3   An example of the use of thumbnails.

 Keep in mind when you design your Web pages that the majority of users are still viewing the Web using a 28.8Kbps modem, so you want to design your pages so that they load quickly.

The thumbnail you create on your page is a miniature version of the larger image file you want the user to view. The thumbnail is a link to the larger file.

FrontPage allows you to easily create thumbnails for any image you want to include on your pages.

To create a thumbnail

1. Create a new page.

2. Insert an image on the page.

3. Make sure you have the Picture toolbar visible. If the Picture toolbar is not visible, select Toolbars from the View menu and make sure Picture is selected.

4. Select the image you inserted and then select the Auto Thumbnail icon on the Picture toolbar. In a second your image is replaced with a thumbnail of the image (see Figure 10.4).

FIGURE **10.4**   A thumbnail version of the original image.

You can also modify how your thumbnails appear on your page. To modify thumbnail appearance

1. From the Tools menu, select Page Options to open the Page Options dialog box.

2. Select the Auto Thumbnail tab to display the Auto Thumbnail sheet (see Figure 10.5).

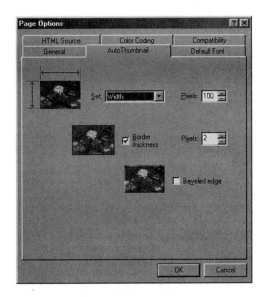

FIGURE 10.5   The Auto Thumbnail sheet of the Page Options dialog box.

3. From here you can control the size of your thumbnails and the size and type of border that will surround your thumbnail images.

CREATING BACKGROUNDS

Another creative use of image files, which may not necessarily fall under the category of "controlling image placement," is using image files for your page backgrounds. There are actually two ways to use image files as backgrounds. You can use an image file to create a normal background, or you can use an image file to create what is called a watermark.

CREATING A NORMAL BACKGROUND

Any image you insert in your pages can also be set as your page background.

To create a background

1. From the File menu, select Properties to open the Page Properties dialog box.

2. Select the Background tab to display the Background sheet (see Figure 10.6).

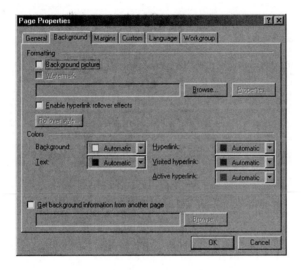

FIGURE **10.6** The Background sheet in the Page Properties dialog box.

3. Select the Background Picture check box and then enter the image you want to use as your background. If you don't remember the exact filename you can browse for it.

4. Select OK and the image you selected is now the background for the page on which you are working (see Figure 10.7).

Most Web designers who use background images try to use small unobtrusive images so that the background takes on a somewhat subtle appearance. You don't want a background image that is going to overpower or compete with the text or images you place in the foreground.

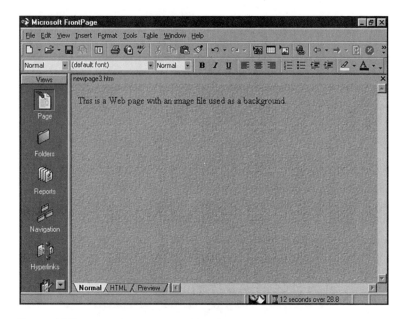

FIGURE 10.7   A Web page with a background image.

CREATING A WATERMARK

You can also set your background image to be a *watermark*. Normally when you use an image as a background, the background image will scroll as the viewer scrolls through the page. But if you set your background image to be a watermark, the background image will remain anchored while the text scrolls over the background.

To set your background image to be a watermark

1. From the File menu, select Properties to open the Page Properties dialog box.

2. Select the Background tab to display the Background sheet.

3. Select the Watermark check box.

4. Select OK and the image you selected for your background is now a watermark.

Keep in mind that watermarks will not work on all Web browsers. If the person viewing your Web page is using a browser other than Netscape or Internet Explorer, the watermarked image will merely appear as a background and will continue to scroll.

In this lesson, you learned how to control image placement on your pages by using tables and thumbnails and how to use image files as Web page backgrounds. In the next lesson, you learn how to use Image Composer to edit your image files.

LESSON 11
USING PHOTODRAW

In this lesson, you learn how to use the PhotoDraw graphics tool.

PHOTODRAW BASICS

PhotoDraw is a graphics utility program that ships with FrontPage. It is an extremely useful tool for editing the graphic files you will want to use on the Web pages you create. PhotoDraw is an excellent tool for editing photographic images but, as you will soon see, can also be used for creating files composed of your images and text you might want to add.

PhotoDraw is an extremely powerful tool. It would be impossible to cover all of its capabilities in this short lesson, but you will see a few of its capabilities—enough to give you a start on how to use this powerful graphics tool.

As a photo-editing tool some of the tasks PhotoDraw will allow you to do include the following:

- Remove dust specks picked up during scanning
- Remove photographic "red-eye" caused by light reflection
- Adjust colors
- Cut and paste objects in the photo
- Add text to your photo images
- Add special effects to your photos
- Add lines, geometric shapes, stars, arrows, and flow charting symbols to your graphics

EDITING IMAGES WITH PHOTODRAW

PhotoDraw really shines as a photo editing tool. Many of the effects and features built into PhotoDraw are designed for working with scanned photographs (JPEG or similar files).

REMOVING SPOTS AND BLEMISHES

Scanned photos are extremely susceptible to dust specks that can appear on the scanned photo no matter how hard you clean the surface of your scanner. You can easily remove any dust specks that end up on your photos with PhotoDraw.

Here's how to remove dust specks or any other irregularities that you want to remove from your photos:

1. Open a photo that contains some dust specks or other types of blemishes such as the apple you see in Figure 11.1 by selecting File, Open.

FIGURE 11.1   A scanned photo with spots and blemishes.

2. On the toolbar, select Touch Up and then select Remove Dust and Spots. The cursor becomes a circle with cross hatching (see Figure 11.2).

FIGURE **11.2** Removing spots and dust specks from the photo.

3. Place the circular cursor on the spot or blemish you want to remove and click once on the spot. The blemish disappears.

4. Repeat step 3 on all of the spots you want to eliminate from your photo. In a few minutes the photo of the image you saw in Figure 11.1 is transformed into the image you now see in Figure 11.3.

What PhotoDraw is doing is sampling the area surrounding the spot and then cloning the surrounding color on top of the blemish. For this reason you can only remove small spots and blemishes.

FIGURE 11.3   The finished product with blemishes removed.

ADJUSTING IMAGE COLORS

PhotoDraw has several functions for changing or adjusting the color of
your images. You can use PhotoDraw to adjust the color balance, brightness, contrast, tint, hue, and saturation. You can also reverse the colors, set
the photo to negative, or remove all color using grayscale.

Working with the unblemished apple from the previous example, let's see
how you can adjust the colors:

1. From the toolbar, select Color and then select Color Balance.

2. Adjust the three sliders and observe how the colors of the apple
   change. You can experiment with these and get some fairly dramatic effects.

3. From the toolbar, select Color and then select Brightness and Contrast.

4. Adjust the two sliders and observe how you can affect the color brightness and color contrast from deep saturation (see Figure 11.4) to complete washout (see Figure 11.5).

FIGURE 11.4   Contrast and brightness showing the depth saturation of colors.

5. You should also try experimenting with Tint, Negative, and Grayscale for some unusual effects.

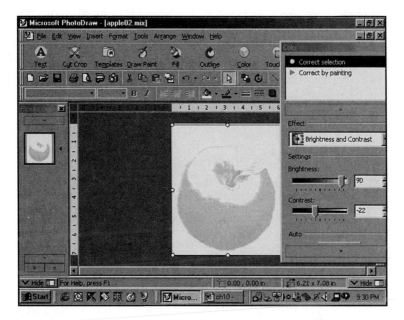

FIGURE 11.5   Contrast and brightness showing a "washed out" effect.

ADDING TEXT WITH PHOTODRAW

PhotoDraw is not just for editing photos. It also includes some spectacular text creation functions.

Here is an example of some of the text creation features you will find in PhotoDraw:

1. Open a new file in PhotoDraw by selecting File, New, Default Picture.

2. From the toolbar, select Text and then select Insert Text. The Text Creation dialog box opens (see Figure 11.6).

FIGURE 11.6   The Text Creation dialog box.

3. In the Text dialog box, change Your text here to the text you want to add to the image or file you are editing. For example, if you want to include your name in the text, change Your text here to your name. You can reposition the text on the file simply by dragging it to any location.

4. If you do not like the default font, size, and style of the text, you can change it by selecting new values in the dialog box.

5. One of the effects you can add to your text is what PhotoDraw calls Bend Text. In the upper portion of the dialog box scroll down until you can select Bend Text to reveal the various text bending options. Select one of the text bending options to alter the shape of your text stream (see Figure 11.7). You can use the Amount slider to adjust the amount of bend in the text.

FIGURE 11.7   Bending your text stream.

6. Another effect possible in PhotoDraw for your text is called
   Designer Text. Scroll up in the dialog box and select Designer
   Text to display the designer text options. When you see a section
   you like, select that designer effect and your text will be transformed according to the designer effect you select (see Figure
   11.8).

The text examples shown here can just as easily be added to a photograph
or any image file you open instead of a new, blank file. Just remember
when you're finished to save your work.

As mentioned earlier, this is just a very small sampling of some of the
features available in PhotoDraw. Feel free to explore and experiment with
the features you have seen in this lesson and the other features available in
PhotoDraw.

FIGURE 11.8   Changing your text to "Designer Text."

In this lesson, you learned about PhotoDraw and some of the image edit-ing capabilities possible by using this utility. In the next lesson, you learn how to use Image Composer, another image editing and composition tool.

Lesson 12

Using Image Composer

In this lesson, you learn how to use the Image Composer graphics tool.

Image Composer Basics

Image Composer is a graphics utility program that ships with FrontPage. Image Composer is a separate program from FrontPage but one that you will find immensely helpful when creating and modifying your Web image files. Image Composer was installed when you installed FrontPage, so you don't have to worry about installing another program on your PC—Image Composer should already be there.

Let's start by getting familiar with Image Composer.

To start Image Composer

1. From the Start menu select Programs, Microsoft Image Composer, Image Composer 1.5.

2. In a few seconds Image Composer appears on your screen (see Figure 12.1).

Across the top of the screen directly under the menu you'll see the Image Composer toolbar. Along the left side of the screen you'll see the Image Composer toolbox (it's pulled away to illustrate here). The toolbox contains most of the common tools you'll use most often in Image Composer—Selection, Arrange, Cutout, Text, Shapes, Paint, Effects, Texture Transfer, Zoom, Pan, Color Tuning (see Figure 12.2).

Toolbox   Toolbar

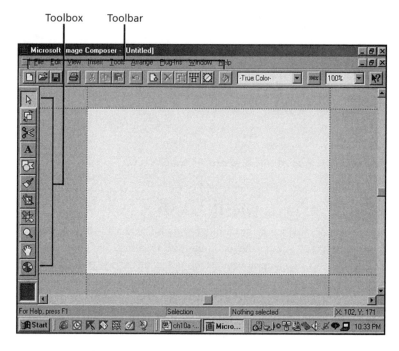

FIGURE 12.1   The Image Composer main screen.

As an image editing tool, Image Composer will allow you to open and modify files in a variety of graphic file formats. Just remember that when you want to use files you create or modify with Image Composer on your Web pages, save them in either the GIF or JPEG file format.

GIF (Graphics Interchange Format) and JPEG (Joint Photographic Experts Group)   The two native file formats used on the World Wide Web.

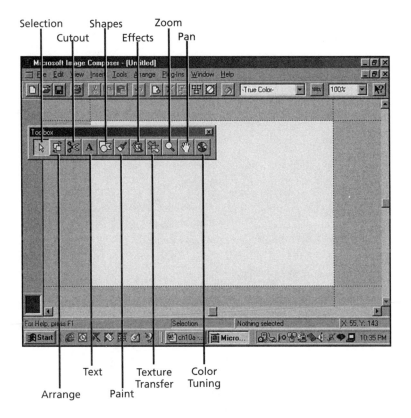

FIGURE 12.2   The Image Composer toolbox.

WORKING WITH IMAGES

One of Image Composer's main strengths is its ability to allow you to edit graphic images you want to use on your Web pages.

Here's an example of some of what you can do with Image Composer:

1. Start Image Composer if it is not already running.

2. Open the file HANDROSE.MIC in the directory ..\Multimedia Files\Photos\Gestures\Microsoft Image Composer\PhotoDisc (see Figure 12.3).

3. Select the Cutout tool from the toolbox. The Cutout dialog box opens (see Figure 12.4).

4. Select the rectangular cutout tool and then drag a rectangle around the bud on the rose. If you need to adjust the rectangle surrounding the bud, you can easily move your cursor to the side of the rectangle you want to adjust and drag that side in or out as needed.

5. Select the Cut Out button in the Cutout dialog box.

6. From the Edit menu, select Copy to make a copy of the rosebud.

7. From the Edit menu, select Paste. Drag the rosebud copy next to the image of the hand holding the rose.

8. The image you just pasted has a circular arrow in the upper-right corner of the image. This circular arrow allows you to rotate the image. Select the circular arrow and rotate the image so that the stem point toward the main image. Drag the image so that it touches the main image.

9. Repeat steps 7 and 8, only place the new image on the other side of the main image. Your edited image should look similar to Figure 12.5.

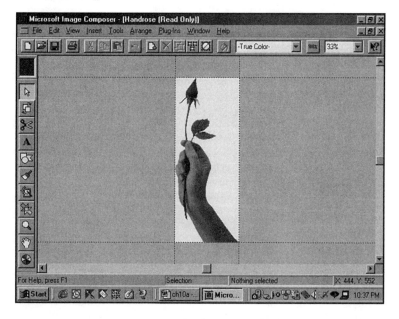

FIGURE 12.3   Image Composer displaying the file HANDROSE.MIC.

FIGURE 12.4   The Cutout dialog box.

FIGURE 12.5   The edited image with additional rosebuds.

This is just a brief example of how you can edit images with Image Composer. Go ahead and try the other tools in the toolbox such as the Shapes tool that you can use to add geometric shapes to your images, or the Paint tool that you can use to "paint over" parts of your images with new colors.

CREATING TEXT WITH IMAGE COMPOSER

Another important feature you will undoubtedly find extremely useful in Image Composer is its text image creation ability.

 Text Image An image file that displays a text message as opposed to a picture of some type.

Rather than explain how you can use Image Composer to create text images, it's easier to show you. Point your browser to http://www.felixnet.com/ and take a look at the title banner across the top of the page. The title banner is a text image created by using Image Composer (see Figure 12.6).

Again, rather than waste time extolling the fancy features and virtues of Image Composer's text creation abilities, let's just jump right in and create a text image.

To create a text image with Image Composer

1. Start Image Composer if it is not already running.

2. Select the Text icon on the toolbox to open the Text dialog box (see Figure 12.7).

3. If you do not like the default values listed in the dialog box for Font, Style, Size, and Color, make whatever changes you like.

4. Click and hold on the work area and drag your cursor to form a rectangle. This rectangle will be the area where your text will appear.

5. Type some text in the rectangular work area. If you can't think of anything in particular, type your name. Select an area outside of the rectangle and your text will appear (see Figure 12.8).

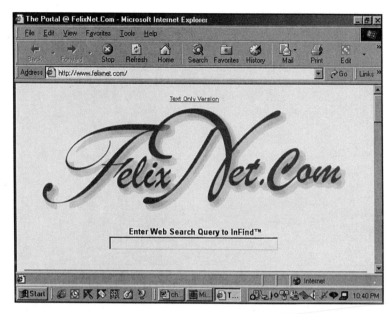

FIGURE **12.6**   A example of the type of text you can create with
Image Composer.

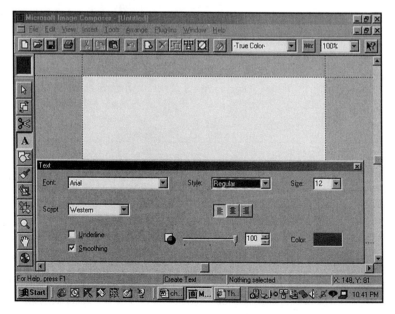

FIGURE **12.7**   The Text dialog box in Image Composer.

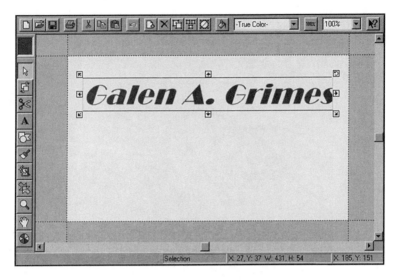

FIGURE 12.8   Example text in Image Composer.

6. Save your image using the Save As command in GIF
   [CompuServe GIF (*.gif)] format. Set the color format to Web
   (Dithered) and make sure you check the Transparent Color
   check box. In most cases you can set the transparent color to
   white (see Figure 12.9).

 Dithering   A technique that smoothes the rough
edges on images so that they do not have "jagged"
edges.

 Transparent Color   Another technique that allows
you to select a single color in your GIF image and
make it appear transparent. Usually you select the
background color in your image file. The result is
when you place the image on your Web page the
image appears to be "cut out" and inserted into your
page.

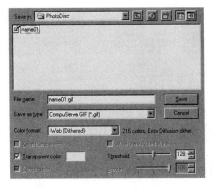

FIGURE 12.9   Saving your text image file.

ADVANCED TEXT EFFECTS

Making text images is a pretty cool trick in and of itself, but that's not all you can do with Image Composer. Image Composer also comes with several dozen special effects that you can apply to the text images you create.

Here's how to dress up your text images with Image Composer's special effects:

1. Select the text image you created earlier in this lesson.

2. From the Tools menu, select Effects to open the Effect dialog box (see Figure 12.10).

FIGURE 12.10   The Effects dialog box in Image Composer.

3. In the Category drop box, select Outlines to bring up the selection of outline effects.

4. Select Drop Shadow and then select the Apply button to apply the drop shadow effect to your text image (see Figure 12.11).

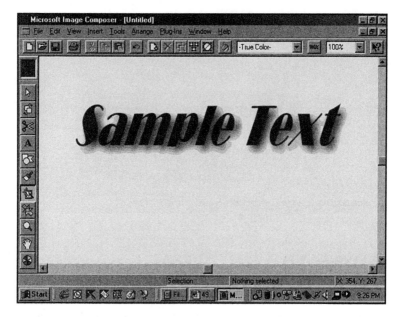

FIGURE 12.11   The drop shadow effect applied to your sample text
image.

This was just one example of the dozens of effects you can apply to your
text images. Feel free to experiment with the different effects until you
find some you like. Note too that on most of the effects, you can select
Details to change the parameters of the effect. Keep in mind while you are
experimenting with each effect that if you do something you don't like,
you can reverse the effect by immediately selecting Undo from the Edit
menu.

In this lesson, you learned how to use the Image Composer graphics tool
to edit your image files and to create text image files. In the next lesson,
you learn how to use the GIF Animator program.

LESSON 13

USING THE GIF ANIMATOR

In this lesson, you learn how to use the GIF animator program to create animated GIF images.

WHAT ARE ANIMATED GIFs?

If you've spent any time surfing the Web, undoubtedly you've seen at least one or two animated GIFs. Animated GIFs usually appear as small image files with some small amount of animation. If you still can't remember seeing one, point your browser to http://www.felixnet.com, scroll down to the bottom of the page, and watch the small "e" in the email icon spin around (see Figure 13.1).

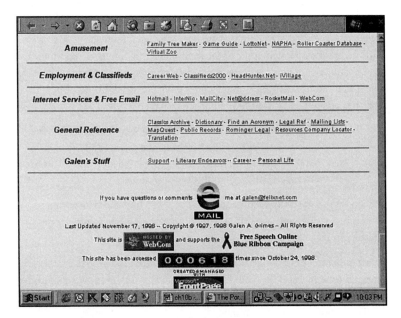

FIGURE 13.1 An example of an animated GIF.

Animated GIFs are essentially a series of individual GIF files stored in a special file format that displays the individual files in whatever order you designate. To create the illusion of animation, each of the individual GIF files is slightly different from the others.

If you've ever seen old-style nickelodeons, you have an idea how animated GIFs work. A nickelodeon was a large wheel and crank with a series of pictures positioned so that when you turned the crank, the wheel turned and flashed the pictures one at a time in rapid succession. Because each picture was slightly different than the previous one, the rotating pictures gave the illusion of animation.

Animated GIFs work on the same principle. The individual GIF files are enclosed in a special animated file format that displays the individual GIF files one at a time in rapid succession.

How to Create Animated GIFs

There are two things you need to create an animated GIF image:

- A series of GIF images, each one slightly different
- The GIF Animator program

You can use either PhotoDraw or Image Composer to create your series of GIF image files. How complex you want the animation to be determines how many GIF images you need to create for your series. You will need to use a minimum of two GIF images. The example you will see in this lesson was created using four individual images (see Figure 13.2).

For the example you are about to see, four GIF image files were created using Image Composer. Each of the files was a text image file of my first name, each in a different color. In two of the files, the text was offset from the other files to help produce the illusion of motion.

Once you get the individual image files you will use to produce your animated image file, you use GIF Animator to assemble them into the animated format.

Essentially what GIF Animator does is display your individual image files one at a time in the order you designate and for a set duration. Most of the time, you will also want the display to repeat itself in a continuous loop so the illusion of motion continues.

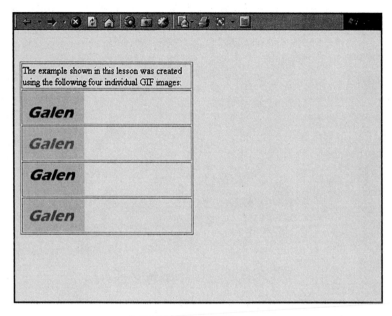

FIGURE 13.2   Four individual GIF image files used in this lesson.

To use GIF Animator

1. Start GIF Animator by selecting Start, Programs, Microsoft Image Composer, Microsoft GIF Animator. In a few seconds the GIF Animator interface appears on your screen (see Figure 13.3).

2. Select the File Open icon on the toolbar, and select the first of your individual image files. The first image should open in the Frame #1 window.

 To identify each of the icons in the Gif Animator toolbar, hold your mouse pointer over each icon. A label will appear identifying the icon in one to two seconds.

3. Select the Insert toolbar icon and select the remaining images, one at a time. The remaining images should appear in the Frame #2, Frame #3, Frame #4, etc. windows (see Figure 13.4).

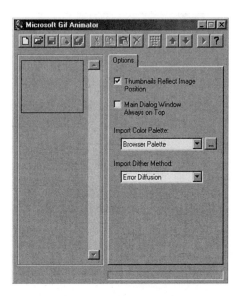

FIGURE 13.3   The GIF Animator main interface.

FIGURE 13.4   The individual GIF files ready to be inserted into the animated file format.

4. After you have your individual images loaded into GIF
   Animator, you can set the animation parameters. Select the
   Animation tab to display the animation settings (see
   Figure 13.5).

FIGURE 13.5   The Animation settings in GIF Animator.

5. Select the Looping check box so that your animation will run
   more than once.

6. Select the Repeat Forever check box to create a continuous animation loop.

7. Select the Image tab to display the image display settings (see
   Figure 13.6).

8. Set the duration parameter for how long you want each individual image to be displayed before the next image is shown. The
   duration is set in hundredths of a second. Keep this number
   small if you want your animation to run quickly. Set a number
   larger if you want to slow down your animation. You will probably have to experiment with the duration setting to find the
   image display duration you like.

9. Test your settings at any time by selecting the Preview toolbar
   icon (see Figure 13.7).

FIGURE 13.6   The Image display settings in GIF Animator.

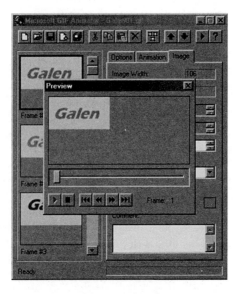

FIGURE 13.7   Previewing your animated GIF.

For some reason, the preview control on GIF Animator does not exactly present the animation the same way it will appear on your Web page. Use the preview control as a guide, not a final arbiter on how your animated GIF will look.

10. When you are satisfied with your animation, select the Save toolbar icon to save your file. The saved file will overwrite the first image file you loaded. If you do not want to overwrite this file, select the Save As icon and give your animated GIF file a different name.

The final test will be how your animated GIF appears on an actual Web page. If you want to see the animated GIF created in this lesson, go to http://www.felixnet.com/gifs/gifs-02.htm (see Figure 13.8).

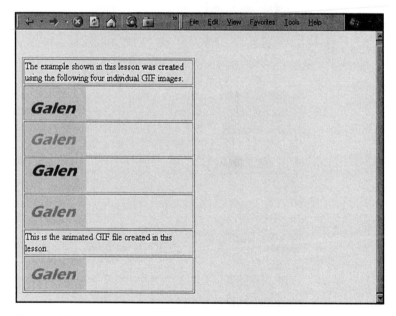

FIGURE 13.8   The animated GIF created in this lesson.

The animated GIF created in this lesson was a fairly simple example of how to use GIF Animator. The only limitations you will face in creating more complex animated GIFs will be your imagination and artistic talents. Just remember the following tips when you are creating animated GIFs:

- Keep the individual images small so they will display quickly and preserve the illusion of animation.

- Keep the number of individual images you use to a minimum. This will help your animation display faster. But if you find the animation appears jerky, you are probably using too few images.

In this lesson, you learned how to use GIF Animator to create animated GIF images for your Web pages. In the next lesson, you learn about creating links in FrontPage.

LESSON 14
CREATING
LINKS

In this lesson, you learn how to create hyperlinks in your Web pages.

HOW LINKS WORK

The key to making things work on the World Wide Web can be summed
up in one word—links. Links (short for "hyperlinks") are the connections
between Web sites and between Web pages.

When you view a page with your browser, the links on that page are inter-
preted by your browser as connections to other files and Internet
resources.

Links can be embedded in either text or images on your pages. Most
browsers make it easy for you to identify links on the pages you view
even if the links are not obvious. Start your browser and go to any page of
your choosing. Move your cursor over any links you see. Notice what
happens? If you are using Netscape or Internet Explorer, your cursor turns
into a hand with a pointing finger. The cursor/finger signifies a link to
another resource on the Internet (see Figure 14.1).

FrontPage not only allows you to create the links you want to embed in
your pages, it also allows you to exercise a fair amount of control over
how your links appear on your pages.

The simplest way to explain what you can do with FrontPage in creating
your links is to take you through the steps of creating and then modifying
a few links. Let's start by creating two links—one to Macmillan
Computer Publishing's Web site and one to the Web site of your author.

To create your links

1. Create a new page.

2. Enter the following text:

   **The first link will go to Macmillan Computer Publishing.
   The second link goes to FelixNet.**

3. Highlight Macmillan Computer Publishing.

4. From the Insert menu, select Hyperlink to open the Create
   Hyperlink dialog box (see Figure 14.2).

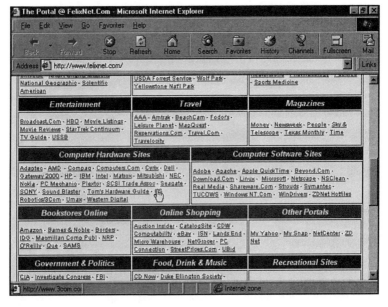

FIGURE 14.1 Your cursor becomes a hand with a pointing finger
when it passes over a link.

5. In the URL: textbox, after the "http://" prefix, enter the following text:

   www.mcp.com

6. Select OK to close the dialog box and save your link.

7. Highlight FelixNet and repeat steps 4 and 5 except enter
   www.felixnet.com in the URL: textbox. Your page should look
   like the example shown in Figure 14.3.

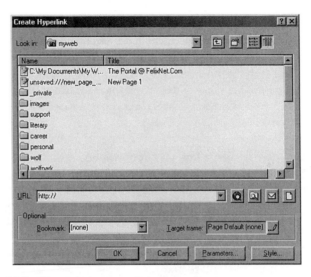

FIGURE **14.2**   The Create Hyperlink dialog box.

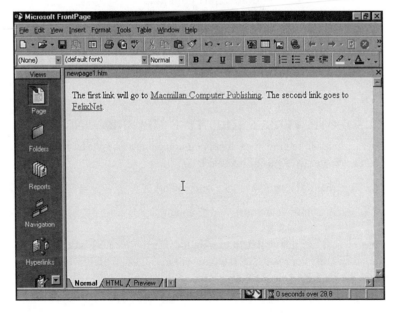

FIGURE **14.3**   How your links will look on your Web pages.

INTERNAL VERSUS EXTERNAL LINKS

When you create a link to another Web page, you can use FrontPage to create either an internal or an external link. An internal link is a link to a page on your Web site. An external link is a link to a page on another Web site. In the previous example in this lesson you made two external links, one to http://www.mcp.com and one to http://www.felixnet.com.

 I didn't make a link to a page! I made it to a site! All Web server software allows what's often referred to as a default start page file. The default start page file is often default.htm or index.htm. When you create a link like http://www.mcp.com without explicitly specifying a filename, the default start page file is automatically displayed. So your link to http://www.mcp.com is actually linking to http://www.mcp.com/default.htm or http://www.mcp.com/index.htm, depending on which is used as the default start page file.

As a rule, external links generally don't require much thought or consideration. If you can display the link with your browser, you can create a link to that page.

ABSOLUTE VERSUS RELATIVE REFERENCING

Internal links do require some thought and planning on your part, because you can create two kinds of internal links:

- Internal links using absolute referencing
- Internal links using relative referencing

Here's a scenario that will help explain the differences. Let's say you've started creating your Web site that you call mysite.com. Figure 14.4 illustrates the progress you've made so far.

Let's say you create the file personal.htm and store it in directory \PERS. To create a link to that file from the file index.htm, you could create the link one of two ways:

- *An absolute link*—http://www.mysite.com/pers/personal.htm

- *A relative link*—../pers/personal.htm

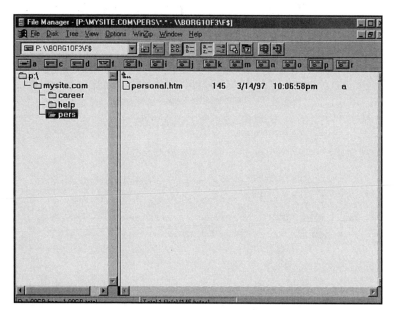

FIGURE **14.4**   Illustration of the directory structure of Web site mysite.com.

The relative link works because both files are stored on the same computer.

Absolute links will always work, but if you change the directory structure of your site or Web server you will have to edit all of your absolute links. When you create your Web site, you should consider using relative links because they give you the flexibility to change your site's directory structure if you ever need to. It may take a little getting used to, but just remember that you need to include enough information for the browser to locate the file called for in the link.

LINKS EMBEDDED IN IMAGE FILES

So far, all of the links you have seen in this lesson have been links embedded in text. You can also embed your links in your image files. You were shown briefly how to embed links in image files back in Lesson 9, "Working with Graphics and Images."

When you create a link embedded in an image file, you need to follow all of the same rules as when you create a link embedded in text.

CREATING BOOKMARKS

Up to this point, all of the links you have seen and created have been links to specific Web pages. These links all open a new page and place the viewer at the top or beginning of the page. But it is also possible to create links that will place viewers at a specific place in your Web pages rather than at the beginning. You need to create links called *bookmarks.*

 Bookmarks　In FrontPage, these are place marker links you create at specific places in your Web pages. Don't confuse these bookmarks with the bookmarks used in Netscape Navigator. Netscape Bookmarks is your listing of Web site URLs that allow you to quickly return to a given site. In Internet Explorer, the comparable term is Favorites. The technical term for FrontPage bookmarks is *named anchors.*

Bookmarks are most commonly used on pages that you have divided into sections of some type, and you want to create a link to the beginning of each section, not just to the beginning of each page.

To create a bookmark

1. Place your cursor at the beginning of the section where you want to place your bookmark.

2. From the Insert menu, select Bookmark to open the Bookmark dialog box (see Figure 14.5).

3. Enter a unique name for your bookmark in the Bookmark Name textbox. When you create other bookmarks, they will appear in the Other Bookmarks on this Page text area.

4. Select OK to create your bookmark and close the dialog box. You will see a bookmark symbol appear on your page where the bookmark is placed (see Figure 14.6).

FIGURE **14.5** The Bookmark dialog box that you use to create FrontPage bookmarks.

Your bookmark is created. Now when you want to create a link to this page and bookmark you will use the following format:

`<url>#<bookmark name>`

For example, if this page is guides.htm and the bookmark you created is called section1, your bookmark link would be the following:

`guides.htm#section1`

bookmark symbol

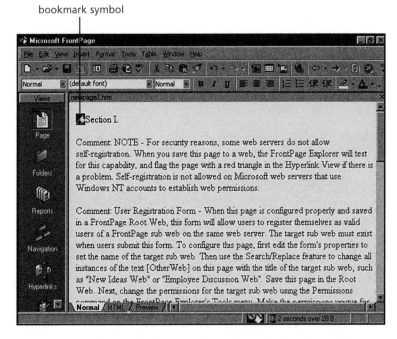

FIGURE 14.6   The bookmark symbol marking the location of the bookmark you just created.

DIFFERENT TYPES OF LINKS

Your links do not have to made to just Web pages. The next most common resources linked to on the Web are files stored on FTP sites.

 FTP   FTP stands for File Transfer Protocol and usually refers to a type of Internet file server used as a large repository for files. Technically speaking, FTP refers to the actual communications protocol used to connect to the server and download or upload (if you have permission) files.

You can create links to files on FTP servers the same way you link to Web pages.

To create an FTP link

1. Create a new page.

2. Enter the text you want to appear as your link.

3. Highlight the text that will become your link to the file on the FTP server.

4. From the Insert menu, select Hyperlink to open the Create Hyperlink dialog box.

5. In the URL: text box, erase the prefix "http://" and type

   ftp://

   followed by the URL of the file to which you are linking. For example, if you are linking to util34.exe on the server ftp.mysite.com in the utility directory, the URL in your link will be **ftp://ftp.mysite.com/utility/util34.exe**.

6. Select OK to close the dialog box.

You can also create links that will trigger the user's email client and pre-address an email message. Most of the time you will create an email link so that users visiting your site can send an email message to you.

Here's how to create an email link:

1. Create a new page.

2. Enter the text you want to appear as your link. You can also create an email link to an image file if you have one that is appropriate, such as at the bottom of the page at http://www.felixnet.com (see Figure 14.7).

3. Highlight the text that will become your email link.

4. From the Insert menu, select Hyperlink to open the Create Hyperlink dialog box.

5. In the URL: text box, erase the prefix "http://" and type the following:

   mailto:

followed by the email address to which you want the user to send the email message. For example, if the email address you want to send the message to is abe_lincoln@logcabin.com, you would enter **mailto:abe_lincoln@logcabin.com** as the URL.

6. Select OK to close the dialog box.

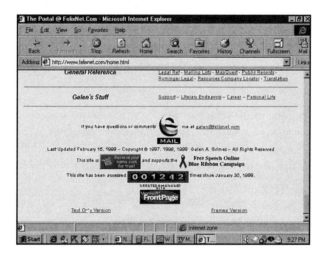

FIGURE 14.7   An email link at *http://www.felixnet.com*.

In this lesson, you learned how to create hyperlinks using FrontPage to Web pages, files on FTP servers, and that allow users to send email messages from your site. In the next lesson, you learn how to use FrontPage to create imagemaps.

LESSON 15
CREATING IMAGEMAPS

In this lesson, you learn what imagemaps are and how to create them for use on your Web pages.

UNDERSTANDING IMAGEMAPS

In Lesson 9, "Working with Graphics and Images," you learned that you can create a link in an image inserted on your Web page. When you create a link in this manner you create only a single link per image.

But you can create multiple links in a single image. When you do this, you create what is called an *imagemap*. Imagemaps contain what are called *hotspots*—areas you designate as links in the image you use to create your imagemap.

Imagemaps are extremely useful on Web pages because they present a graphical illustration for viewers to use to navigate through your Web site. Your main concern in creating an imagemap is selecting an image that is simple to follow and aids your navigation efforts.

CREATING IMAGEMAPS WITH FRONTPAGE

The first step in creating an imagemap is selecting the image you are going to use. Because GIF and JPEG image files are native to the Web and can be read by all browsers, you are encouraged to choose a file in one of these two formats. You also want to select an image file that is relatively small and will be loaded quickly by the user's browser.

So what makes a good imagemap? A good imagemap is any image that makes it easy to navigate around your Web site. You can use images of actual maps. You can also use images that contain text. Think of some of the sites you have visited where you have seen and used imagemaps and try to remember whether they helped or hindered your efforts to navigate through the site.

If you are good with any of the multitude of graphics programs on the market, you may even consider creating your own image files. Just remember to save them as either .GIF or .JPG files.

Once you've selected the file you are going to use, here is what you do to turn the file into an imagemap:

1. Insert the image file you want to use for your imagemap into your Web page imagemap (see Figure 15.1).

FIGURE 15.1   A sample image that can be used to create an imagemap.

2. Select the image you inserted on your page.

3. Make sure you have the Picture toolbar displayed. From the Picture toolbar, select the Polygonal Hotspot icon. Your cursor should change shape to resemble a small pencil.

If you are not sure which icon to select on a toolbar simply pass, or hover, the cursor over each icon for a few seconds. The name of the icon will be displayed.

4. You want to use the pencil shaped cu.sor to trace around the outside edge of an object in your image. Each object you select will be one of your imagemap's hotspots. Select, or more precisely, click in a corner of an object and an anchor (square) appears. Move your cursor to the next corner in line around the object and you can see the hotspot being traced around the object (see Figure 15.2). Select or click in each corner where you want to change the direction of your object tracing and a new anchor appears.

FIGURE 15.2   Tracing around the area of the image, creating a hotspot.

5. Continue tracing around the object creating anchors until you reach the point where you began. Select the first anchor again to complete the tracing around the object, and the Create Hyperlink dialog box appears (see Figure 15.3).

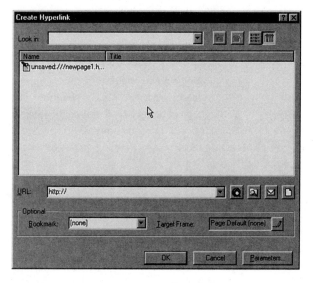

FIGURE 15.3   The Create Hyperlink dialog box.

6. Enter the page you want to link to in the URL textbox. Select OK to save your link and close the dialog box.

7. Repeat steps 3–6 for as many objects in your image that you want to turn into imagemap hotspots (see Figure 15.4).

If the areas of your image are regular in shape, either square or circular, you can select either the Circular Hotspot icon or the Rectangular Hotspot icon instead of the Polygonal Hotspot icon. These tools do not require that you trace around the areas of your image you want to turn into hotspots. Instead, you merely select the hotspot icon tool you want to use and select the area of the image you want to turn into a hotspot (see Figure 15.5).

Regardless of which hotspot icon tool you select, you can resize the hotspot by selecting one of the anchors and dragging until the hotspot is either larger or reshaped to your liking.

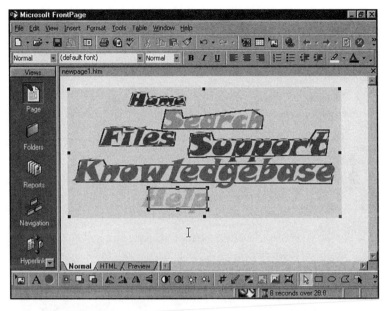

FIGURE **15.4**   Multiple hotspots created on an image file.

FIGURE **15.5**   Rectangular and circular hotspots.

PREVIEWING YOUR IMAGEMAP

You will need to use the Preview tab in FrontPage to test your imagemap.

To preview your imagemap

1. Make sure you are still viewing the page you just created. If the page is not visible, select the Page icon on the Views bar.

2. Make sure also that the Normal tab is selected at the bottom of the Page view.

3. To preview your page and the imagemap you just created, select the Preview tab and you will see your page as it will be viewed with a Web browser.

4. Move your cursor over the areas of the image where you created hotspots. If your links are working, the cursor should change to a small hand when it passes over a link (see Figure 15.6).

FIGURE 15.6   Previewing your imagemap.

The Preview tab is not just for previewing pages with imagemaps. You can use the Preview tab to preview any page you create with FrontPage, regardless of the types of links you create in it.

As you can see, imagemaps are a snap to create using FrontPage. Just make sure that when you select an image to use as an imagemap, you select an image that will visually add to your Web page. And be sure it's easy for the viewers who see your page to figure out which hotspot links will help them navigate to their desired pages.

In this lesson, you learned how to create imagemaps. In the next lesson, you learn how to use and create frames.

LESSON 16

WORKING WITH FRAMES

In this lesson, you learn about frames and how to use them on your Web pages.

UNDERSTANDING FRAMES

In Lesson 4, "Getting Started Using FrontPage Templates," you learned that FrontPage includes over two dozen Web page templates that you can use to build fairly complex Web pages. If you spent any time looking over those templates, you may have noticed that some of them allow you to easily create Web pages using frames (see Figure 16.1).

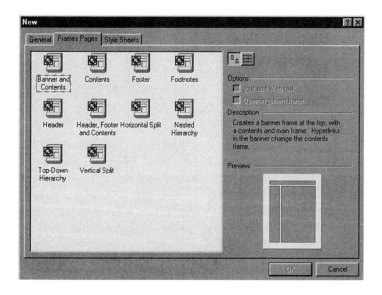

FIGURE 16.1   FrontPage's frame creation templates.

Frames essentially are independent Web pages displayed on one screen (see Figure 16.2).

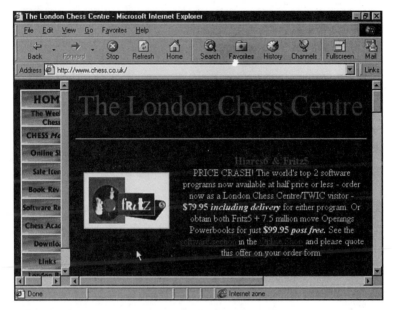

FIGURE 16.2   An example of a page using frames.

Each of the framed areas is a separate HTML file or page, and each area or page is independent of the other areas or pages. Each framed area can change without affecting the other areas, or each framed area can scroll independently of the other framed areas. You often see pages utilizing frames with heavy borders surrounding or dividing each of the framed areas, but frames also can be displayed borderless.

SHOULD YOU USE FRAMES?

You should be aware that despite the potential flexibility offered by the use of frames, not everyone on the Web is a big fan of frames. There are as many people who swear at frames as there are who swear by them.

When frames were first introduced, not all browsers could display them as they were intended to be viewed. There have also been problems with some sites that use frames with the frames "carrying over" into other sites.

Since any page can be displayed in a frame, it is not uncommon for you to be viewing a site using frames and then attempting to jump to a new site (which is not using frames). Instead of the new site displaying fully in your browser, you may see the new site appear inside one of the frames.

Another problem often mentioned when the discussion turns to frames is that not all sites using frames display properly at different screen resolutions. For example, a Web page at 800×600 or at 1024×768 may not display properly to someone who is viewing the Web at a screen resolution of 640×480.

If you are intent on using frames, these warnings and cautions should not deter you. Just be aware of some of the pitfalls you can encounter along the way.

CREATING FRAMES USING FRONTPAGE TEMPLATES

Your first step after deciding to use frames on your site is to sketch on paper how you want your site to look. You also should plan how you want your site to operate. Do you want your framed areas to scroll or remain stationary? Do you plan to place a menu or navigation bar in one of the frames?

After you have planned your use of frames, look over the templates available in FrontPage and see if there is one that closely resembles the plan you have devised. When you are just starting out with frames, it is best to keep their use simple until you become more familiar with them. Try using a template containing only two frames until you become comfortable with frames.

Let's step through setting up a very simple site using frames and you can get an idea of what's involved.

To create a page with frames

   1. From the File menu, select New, Page to open the New page dialog box.

2. Select the Frames Pages tab to display the Frames Pages sheet
   and the Frames templates (see Figure 16.3).

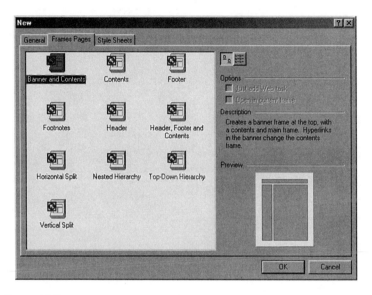

FIGURE 16.3   FrontPage's frame templates choices.

3. Select the frame you want to use for your page. For this example, select the Contents template, which will create a page with
   two frame areas.

4. Select OK to close the dialog box and create your page using the
   template you selected (see Figure 16.4).

At this point you need to decide what you want to place in each of your
frames. You can take existing pages and "frame" them or you can create
new pages from scratch.

For this example, you create a simple menu in the small frame on the left.
The menu is comprised of three links. Each link displays a different page
in the frame on the right.

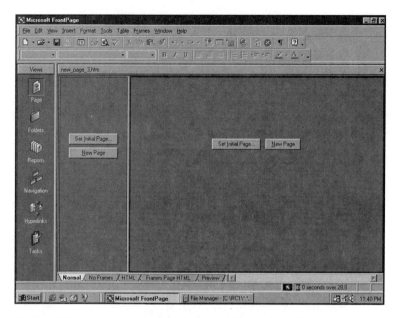

FIGURE 16.4   A page using the Contents frame template.

To create the simple menu

1. In the left frame, select the New Page button and a new page is created in the frame.

2. Type the following text in the framed page:

    Page 1

    Page 2

    Page 3

3. Select the text Page 1. From the Insert menu, select Hyperlink to open the Create Hyperlink dialog box.

4. In the URL textbox enter the name of one of the pages you created in one of the previous lessons.

5. Select the Change Target Frame button next to the Target Frame textbox to open the Target Frame dialog box (see Figure 16.5).

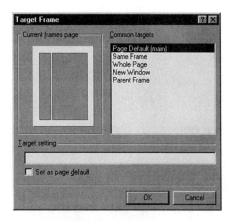

FIGURE 16.5   The Target Frame dialog box.

6. The Target Frame dialog box displays a representation of the frames on your page. In the representation, select the framed area on the right by clicking inside the frame. This is where your linked page will be displayed when you select the link you are creating.

7. Select OK to close the Target Frame dialog box. Select OK again to close the Create Hyperlink dialog box.

8. Repeat steps 3–7 selecting the text Page 2 and Page 3 and selecting two different pages to be displayed by these links just as you did for the link Page 1.

9. Your framed page is almost completed. All you need to do to complete your page is select the page that will be displayed in the right frame initially when your page is displayed. Most often you will select the same page called by the link Page 1. Select the Set Initial Page button in the frame on the right to open the Create Hyperlink dialog box.

10. Enter the name of the file linked to the Page 1 link back in step 4.

11. Select OK to close the dialog box.

12. From the File menu, select Save to save your files. You are prompted to save all of the files you created. Because you

created the file appearing in the left frame, you are prompted to save that file and the file called the frameset file, which controls the entire framed page.

13. After you've saved your files, select the Preview tab to display your framed page (see Figure 16.6) and test the frame controls.

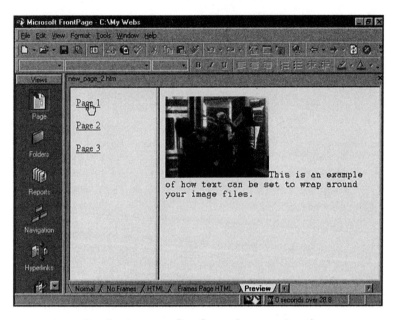

FIGURE 16.6   Previewing your first framed page using the FrontPage Preview feature.

Even though frames have been around for a few years, they are still somewhat controversial. Some Web designers like to use them, and some Web designers have absolute disdain for frames. You can't please everyone, but you can minimize the criticism you might receive from the anti-frame crowd. If you decide to use frames in your Web site, make sure the use of frames is justified and then try to keep your frames to a minimum.

This lesson showed you how to create a simple page divided into two frames and how to create links to display different pages in one of the frames. Your use of frames is limited only by your imagination. Just remember—don't go overboard using frames. When using frames the old maxim "a little is good, a lot is better" usually doesn't apply.

In this lesson, you learned how to work with frames. In the next lesson, you learn how to publish your site on a Web Server and how to administer it.

LESSON 17

PUBLISHING AND ADMINISTERING YOUR WORK

In this lesson, you learn how to publish your Web on a Web server and how to administer your site.

PREPARING TO PUBLISH YOUR WEB

You've spent the last 16 lessons learning how to create your Web site using the various tools available in FrontPage. That's all well and good, but your work is for naught if you are the only one who can see your site. To make your site available to others you need to publish it on a Web server—either a Web server on your corporate intranet or a Web server on the Internet.

Publishing your Web is incredibly easy using FrontPage. All you do is select the Web you want to publish and then select where you want it published; FrontPage does all the work.

But before you can publish your Web there are a few tasks you need to do.

First, you need to make sure that you have a functioning Web server, either on the Internet or on your company's intranet. A Web server is necessary so that others can view your work. There are numerous companies that produce Web server software you can use, and almost all will work satisfactorily.

Second, you need to make sure you have the necessary security or access rights that will enable you to create or copy your files to the Web server. Web servers typically allow users what is called "read-only" access, which allows them to view but not modify files on the server. To publish your Web to the server, you will need read, write, create, and delete rights to the server. The server administrator is responsible for granting you the proper access rights that permit you to publish your work.

Third, you need to make sure that the Web server you are publishing to has the FTP service operating. FTP is the communications protocol FrontPage uses to connect to and copy your files to the server.

And while it is not essential, it will be helpful to have the Microsoft FrontPage server extensions installed on the server. The FrontPage server extensions allow you to utilize some of the advanced features in FrontPage, such as active elements (covered in Lesson 19, "Using the FrontPage Active Elements").

UPLOADING YOUR WEB TO A SERVER

FrontPage uses the File Transfer Protocol (FTP) to connect to and upload your files to the designated file server. As long as the FTP service is functioning on your Web server, you don't need to make any configuration changes or settings to FrontPage to publish your Webs.

To publish your Web to your Web server

1. Select and open the Web you want to publish.

2. From the File menu, select Publish Web to open the Publish Web dialog box (see Figure 17.1).

FIGURE 17.1   The FrontPage Publish Web dialog box.

3. In the Specify the Location to Publish your FrontPage Web to: text box enter the URL of the Web server where you want to publish your Web. You can designate either the FTP or HTTP protocol in the URL. For example, if you are publishing to a

Web server in the MyCompany.Com domain, you could enter the URL as either **http://www.mycompany.com** or **ftp://ftp.mycompany.com.**

 While most Web servers have the computer name www (as in www.mycompany.com) and most ftp servers have the corresponding ftp computer name (such as ftp.mycompany.com), these are not hard-and-fast rules, so don't assume your servers have these names. You can check with your server's administrator to get the computer name for your server.

4. Select the Publish button to begin uploading your Web to your server.

 The first time you publish your Web, it doesn't matter if you select the Publish Changed Pages Only check box since nothing has changed. On subsequent updates to your site, selecting this check box can significantly improve your update times, especially if you are working on a large site with hundreds or even thousands of pages.

5. Depending on the size of your Web and the speed of your connection, publishing can take anywhere from a few seconds to a few minutes (see Figure 17.2). When FrontPage has completed publishing your Web, and if publishing was successful, it will display a message similar to the one you see in Figure 17.3.

6. To preview your just published site, select the link Click Here to View Your Published Web Site (see Figure 17.4).

7. Select the Done button to close the FrontPage Publish Web dialog box.

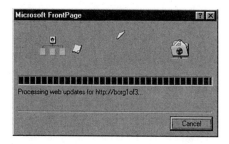

FIGURE 17.2 Publishing your Web to a Web server.

FIGURE 17.3 FrontPage indicating that publishing was successful.

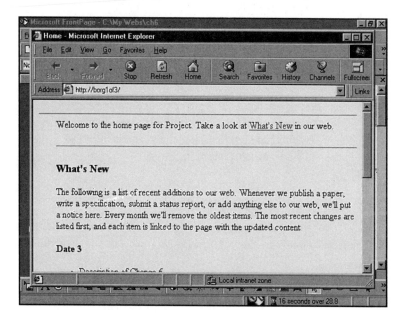

FIGURE 17.4 Previewing your just published Web.

TENDING TO ADMINISTRATION DUTIES ON YOUR SITE

Administering your site consists mainly of adding or updating pages to your Web. As you use FrontPage to modify your Web, you don't have to worry about remembering what folder you place which file into. FrontPage takes care of that task for you. When you publish your Web, FrontPage will keep all of the files composing your Web in just the right order.

FrontPage is also smart enough to know which files you have modified and which files you have added since you last published your Web. When you are ready to update your Web, you merely publish your Web just as you did before.

To update your published Web

1. Make sure the Web you want to update is open.

2. From the File menu, select Publish Web to open the FrontPage Publish Web dialog box.

3. In the Specify the Location to Publish Your FrontPage Web to: text box, enter the URL of the Web server where you published your Web. Make sure the Publish Changed Pages Only check box is selected.

4. Select the Publish button to begin uploading your new and/or updated pages to your server. FrontPage is smart enough to compare your published Web to the Web on your computer and upload only the new or changed pages.

CHECKING YOUR HYPERLINKS

In addition to making it easier to update your Web site when you add or change pages, FrontPage also has the capability to check your hyperlinks.

To check your hyperlinks

1. Open the Web you want to check.

2. From the Tools menu, select Recalculate Hyperlinks to open the Recalculate Hyperlinks dialog box (see Figure 17.5).

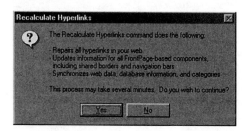

FIGURE **17.5**   You can use the Recalculate Hyperlinks feature to check the links in your Webs.

3. Select Yes to begin checking the hyperlinks in your Web. Depending on the number of links contained in your Web, this check can take anywhere from a few seconds to a few minutes.

REPORTING ON YOUR WEB SITE

Another administrative duty you might want to get into the habit of performing is running the reporting feature on your Webs. The reporting feature can give you a very detailed overview of your Webs.

To obtain a report on your Web

1. Open the Web for which you want to obtain a report.

2. From the Views Bar, select the Reports icon. Your report appears on your screen in a few seconds (see Figure 17.6).

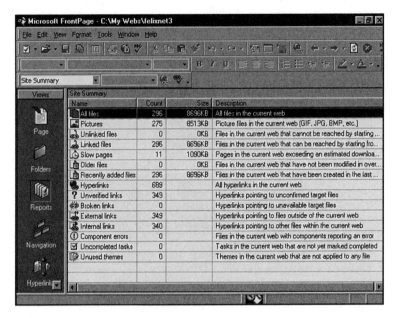

FIGURE 17.6   A typical Web report.

In this lesson, you learned how to publish your Webs to the Internet and how to administer your Web site. In the next lesson, you learn how to add multimedia audio and video files to your Web pages.

LESSON 18

ADDING MULTIMEDIA AND ANIMATION TO YOUR SITE

In this lesson, you learn how to add multimedia sound and animation files to your Web site.

DEFINING MULTIMEDIA

You learned how to enhance your Web site by adding graphic images in previous lessons. Up to this point, these images were all static images. But FrontPage does not limit you to using only static images and files on your Web pages. FrontPage also enables you to add multimedia video and audio to your pages.

Adding multimedia audio and video files will make your site more interesting, but bear in mind that these enhancements come with a price. To hear any audio files you add to your site, viewers will need an audio-equipped PC—a PC with a soundcard and speakers. Also, if you plan to add multimedia video clips to your site, these files are typically quite large and incur a long download time.

ADDING SOUND TO YOUR PAGES

Adding sound to your Web pages with FrontPage is a snap. The hardest problem you may encounter is simply locating or creating the sound files you want to use.

To see (or more precisely, to hear) how sound can be used as an enhancement to your pages, start your browser and jump to http://www.prs.net/midi.html.

If you don't hear anything, make sure you have a soundcard installed in your PC and you have speakers that are turned on. Also, check that the volume control is turned up.

The Classical MIDI Archives site is one of several dozen sites on the Internet where you can select and enjoy classical music in MIDI format.

 MIDI   MIDI stands for Musical Instrument Digital Interface, and is an electronic representation of sounds and music as opposed to a digitally stored recording. Because MIDI files are not actually sound recordings but instead representations of sound, MIDI files tend to be substantially smaller in file size than digital recordings. This factor has contributed largely to the popularity of MIDIs on the Internet.

Because MIDI files are fairly small in size, they appear to begin playing almost automatically. In reality, the files do not begin playing until your browser has downloaded them to your PC. If you look in the file cache directory on your PC (c:\Program Files\... for Internet Explorer and c:\Program Files\Netscape\Users\<user name>\cache for Netscape) you will see one or more files with the file extension .MID. These are the MIDI files you have been listening to.

 Some versions of the same browser can place your temporary Internet files in different directories. If you're having trouble locating your MIDI files, use the Find utility and search for files with the extension .MID.

Even though your browser will download a MIDI file to your PC before you can listen to it, if you intend to use any files downloaded make sure you have permission from the owner first. Many MIDI files, just like JPEG and GIF image files, are copyrighted and are not yours for the taking.

Once you've located (and obtained the necessary permissions) one or more MIDI files you want to use on your site, you might find it easier if you store them in a separate directory like you do your image files. If you store your image files in an \IMAGES directory, you might want to create a \AUDIO directory to store your MIDI files in.

To add a MIDI or other type of multimedia audio file to your site

1. Select and open the page to which you want to add your audio file.

2. From the File menu, select Properties to open the Page Properties dialog box (see Figure 18.1).

3. In the Background Sound section, enter the name of your audio file in the Location text box. Use the Browse button if you cannot remember where the file is stored.

4. In the Loop section, determine how many times you want the audio file to play. You can select Forever, which means the file will play over and over again as long as the page it is inserted on is displayed. Or you can select the exact number of times you want the audio file to play.

5. Select OK to save your page properties and close the dialog box.

6. To preview your page with its background audio, select the Preview tab to display the page.

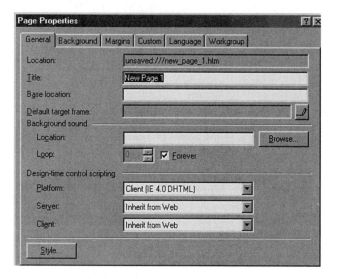

FIGURE 18.1   The FrontPage Page Properties dialog box.

ADDING VIDEO CLIPS TO YOUR PAGES

FrontPage also has tools for allowing you to add video clips to your Web pages. As stated earlier, adding video to your site incurs a price from your viewers. Video clips tend to be very large files and most often need to be downloaded by your viewers before they can be seen.

 Just as with MIDI audio files, many video clips you encounter on the Web are copyrighted. Make sure you obtain the proper permissions before using someone else's video clips on your site.

If you are serious about adding multimedia video clips to your site and intend to do it on a large scale, you need to invest in the resources needed to provide what is called *streaming video*. Streaming video is a way to provide video clips to your viewers without making them incur the time involved in downloading large video files. Like the name implies, streaming video is delivered to your viewers in a steady stream, and your viewers can actually watch the video as it is being delivered to them. Streaming video most often requires some sort of video delivery system on the Web server and some type of receiver or player that the viewer needs to obtain and install to view the streaming video you are delivering. One of the most popular streaming delivery systems is from Real Media at http://www.real.com.

To add a video clip to your site

1. Select and open the page to which you want to add your video clip.

2. From the Insert menu, select Picture, Video to open the Video dialog box so you can select the video clip file you want to insert (see Figure 18.2).

Pay attention to the type of video file you are inserting. Windows (95/98/NT) includes viewers for several types of video file formats (.AVI, MOV, and so on), but if you select a video file format that cannot be played by the standard Windows Media Player, be sure to either include the viewer or provide a link to a site where the viewer can be obtained. An example is the QuickTime format from Apple (http://www.apple.com).

FIGURE 18.2   Inserting a video file onto your page.

3. By default, FrontPage will set all video clips to start automatically when the page they are inserted in is opened. If you do not want your video clip to automatically start when the page is opened, select the object on the page and then select Properties from the Format menu to open the Picture Properties dialog box. If the Video sheet is not displayed, select the Video tab to display that sheet (see Figure 18.3).

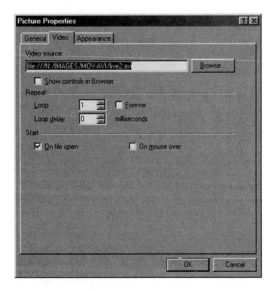

FIGURE 18.3   The Video sheet in the Picture Properties dialog box.

4. There are three options for automatically starting your video clip—when the page is opened, when the mouse pointer is passed over the onscreen clip, or by including onscreen controls for the user. Select the start method you want to use for your clip by selecting one or more of the three check boxes.

5. You can also select how many times you want the clip to play by entering a number in the Loop counter. If you select to repeat the clip, you can also select how long a delay you want to place between each successive playing of the clip.

6. When you have finished making changes in how you want to the clip to play, select OK to save your changes and close the dialog box.

7. To preview your clip, select the Preview tab (see Figure 18.4).

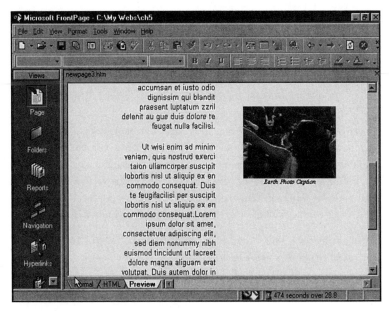

FIGURE 18.4   A video clip playing on a Web page.

In this lesson, you learned how to add multimedia audio and video clips to your Web pages. In the next lesson, you learn how to use FrontPage's active elements.

LESSON 19

USING THE FRONTPAGE ACTIVE ELEMENTS

In this lesson, you learn how to incorporate some of FrontPage's active elements into your Web pages.

UNDERSTANDING FRONTPAGE ACTIVE ELEMENTS

FrontPage active elements are a set of tools included with FrontPage that enable you to add a splash of pizzazz and user interaction to your Web sites.

Hover buttons are one of the most popular active elements in FrontPage, and they allow you to add certain special effects to navigation buttons you might want to create. For example, suppose on your main page you create a set of hover buttons to help users navigate to various sections of your site. Let's say you create navigation links to your Support section, your Download section, and to your Personal section (see Figure 19.1).

If you create these links using active element hover buttons, you can set the buttons to glow when a user passes his or her mouse over the button, play sounds, or display selected images.

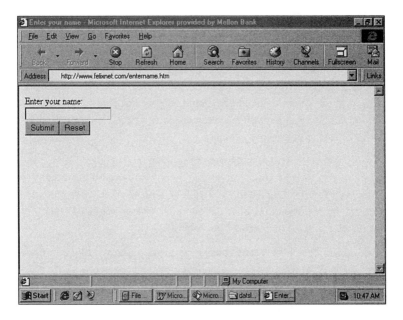

FIGURE 19.1   A sample Web page using hover buttons for navigation.

 Many of the active elements in FrontPage are written in a special programming language called Java. You don't have to worry about learning programming or learning Java to create hover buttons, but you should be aware that for the active elements to function correctly the browser used by people who visit your site needs to support Java. Fortunately Netscape and Internet Explorer both support Java and nearly 90–95 percent of users on the World Wide Web use one of these two browsers.

In addition to hover buttons, you can also use FrontPage's active elements to create *hit counters* and *marquees*. A hit counter is a display device that shows how many people have visited your site. A marquee is a scrolling text banner. Both of these will be explained in this lesson.

CREATING HOVER BUTTONS

As mentioned earlier, hover buttons are one of the most widely used and popular of FrontPage's active elements. Hover buttons are used primarily to create special effect links to other sites or pages. You create your hover buttons to use any of the colors available on your PC, and you can make your hover buttons glow using a variety of glow effects. You can also add sound effects to your hover buttons.

Hover buttons are written in the Java programming language. You don't have to worry about learning programming or learning Java but, because of the way Java is designed to work with Web browsers, to test your hover buttons you will need to publish them to your Web server (see Lesson 17, "Publishing and Administering Your Work").

In this example you see how to create navigation links by using hover buttons. You will be creating navigation links from a main page to three different pages using hover buttons.

To create hover buttons

1. Open a new page.

2. From the Insert menu, select Component, Hover Button to open the Hover Button Properties dialog box (see Figure 19.2).

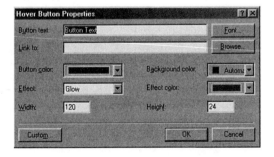

FIGURE **19.2**   The Hover Button Properties dialog box used for creating hover buttons.

3. In the Button Text text box, enter the text label you want to appear on your hover button. For this example enter **Support Site**. If you want to change the font style or font size that appears on your button, select the Font button and select the style and size you want to use.

4. In the Link To text box, enter the URL of the site or page to which you want this hover button to link. In this example, you create a link to Macmillan Computer Publishing's Web site, so enter **http://www.mcp.com**.

5. If you want to change the button's default color scheme or the default effect (glow), you can make those changes from the various drop boxes. You can usually tell what most of the button effects do by their names—glow, reverse glow, bevel out, bevel in, and so on. Don't be afraid to experiment with each effect. You can also change the size of the button you create by changing the default values for width and height.

6. If you want to add sound effects to your hover button, select the Custom button to open the Custom dialog box (see Figure 19.3). You can use almost any type of sound file (.wav, .mid, .au, and so on). Just remember to use small files because they will be downloaded along with your page to the PC viewing the page. You might also want to test the files by using the Microsoft Media Player first to make sure they will work in Windows. You can set the sound file to begin playing either when the person viewing your page clicks on the hover button or merely passes (hovers) his or her mouse over the button.

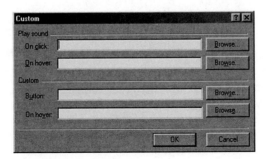

FIGURE 19.3   The Custom dialog box used for adding sound effects and images to your hover buttons.

7. When you have completed setting the values for your hover button, select OK to save, close the dialog box, and return to your page.

8. Repeat steps 2–7, creating hover buttons with the labels **Download** and **Personal**. Make your Download button link to **http://www.tucows.com**, and make your Personal button link to your own personal page (for example, **personal.htm**). Your three buttons should look similar to the three hover buttons displayed in Figure 19.4.

 If you want to create your three hover buttons side by side instead of in a vertical column, you might consider creating a one row table with three columns. You can adjust the width of the table to accommodate your three buttons and you can then hide the table (border=0).

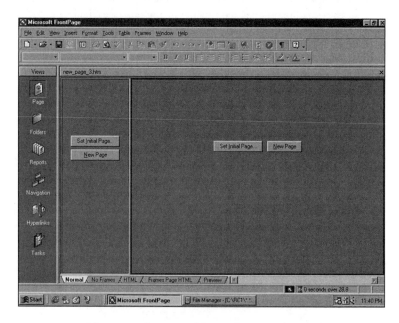

FIGURE **19.4**   Three newly created hover buttons for navigating through a Web site.

9. Save and then publish your page to your Web server (see Lesson 17). When you view your page, it should look similar to the page displayed in Figure 19.5.

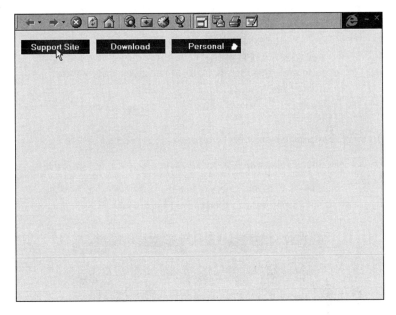

FIGURE 19.5   The hover buttons created in this example published to a Web server use the glow effect.

CREATING MARQUEES

If you are an old-time Windows user who started with version 3.1 or earlier, you should be familiar with marquees. One of the most popular screen-savers used in earlier versions of windows was the marquee screen-saver. In many companies, it was a very common sight to see PC after PC during the lunch hour to have a scrolling banner on the screen stating that the user was "...out to lunch..." and what time to expect the user's imminent return.

Well, the seemingly ubiquitous scrolling marquee messages are still around, only now you can incorporate them into your Web pages by using FrontPage.

Unlike hover buttons, marquees are not Java programs. They are, instead, an HTML addition created by Microsoft. Unfortunately, not every browser manufacturer has modified its product to recognize marquees. Netscape, for instance, will not recognize and display FrontPage-generated marquees. Internet Explorer will. If you decide to incorporate a marquee message in your Web site, be aware that not everyone will be able to see it.

To create a marquee banner on your page

1. Open the page in which you want to insert your marquee banner.

2. From the Insert menu, select Component, Marquee to open the Marquee Properties dialog box (see Figure 19.6).

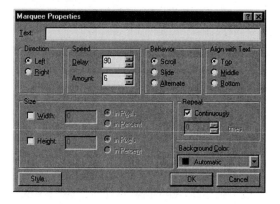

FIGURE 19.6   The Marquee Properties dialog box used for creating marquee messages in your Web pages.

3. In the Text text box, enter the message you want to display in your marquee banner. While you can enter what may start to seem like an endless stream of text, you should limit your marquee message to the amount of text that can easily fit on the screen at one time.

4. You can also control other factors of your marquee such as the speed and direction your message travels, font and text attributes, its behavior and alignment, and its size and color. You can also determine if you want your marquee to scroll continuously or a set number of times.

5. When you have completed configuring your marquee banner, select OK to save your settings and close the dialog box.

6. To preview your marquee, select the Preview tab (see Figure 19.7).

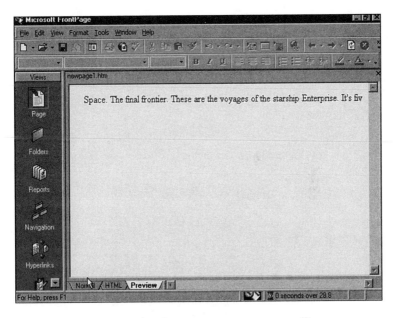

FIGURE 19.7   An example of a marquee message scrolling across a Web page.

HIT COUNTERS

Hit counters employ an odometer style counter on your screen and keep a running tab of the number of visitors who have visited your site. Hit counters are a little more difficult to implement because you not only have to insert the proper instructions into your page, but the server you are running your site on also has to have installed a special set of server-based extension programs from Microsoft.

Not every Web server administrator has taken the time to install Microsoft's FrontPage server extensions, but a large percentage have. If you are publishing to a commercial Web server hosting company, it is a good possibility that they have or can provide the FrontPage server extensions. If you create a hit counter and it doesn't work, you might want to ask your server administrator if the server extensions have been installed. If they haven't, ask if they can be installed.

To create a hit counter on your page

1. Open the page on which you want to place your hit counter.

2. Position your cursor where you want the hit counter to be inserted.

3. From the Insert menu, select Component, Hit Counter to open the Hit Counter Properties dialog box (see Figure 19.8).

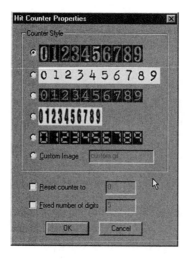

FIGURE 19.8   The Hit Counter Properties dialog box used for inserting hit counters in your pages.

4. Select the type of hit counter you want to create by selecting the appropriate radio button in front of the available choices.

5. Select if you want to reset the counter to some number other than 0 and if you want to set the number of digits in the counter to more or less than 5.

6. Select OK to save your selection and close the dialog box.

7. Save the page with your hit counter and publish it to your Web server.

8. To preview your page with its hit counter, open the page in your browser (see Figure 19.9).

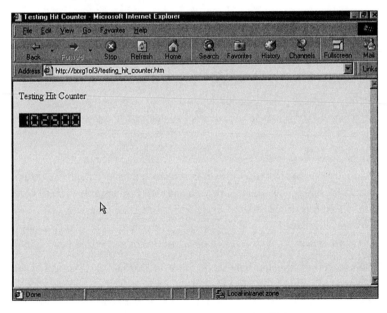

FIGURE 19.9   A sample hit counter on a sample Web page.

In this lesson, you have learned how to use some of FrontPage's active elements—hover buttons, marquees, and hit counters. In the next lesson, you learn how to work with style sheets.

LESSON 20

WORKING WITH STYLE SHEETS

In this lesson, you learn about style sheets, how to create them, and how and when to use them.

UNDERSTANDING STYLE SHEETS

What would you do if you had spent the last month setting up your company's Web site and posting information on several hundred pages, and then one morning your boss came up and said she wanted you to change the font on the entire site from Times Roman to Arial?

Before you start planning your boss's demise, let me introduce you to style sheets and how you can accomplish this task in a few minutes instead of several days.

Style sheets, officially called *Cascading Style Sheets* but known informally by everyone as simply style sheets, are a means to control certain attributes throughout your entire Web site. Style sheets allow you to control all aspects of the text appearing on your pages—font, size, color, and any set attributes. But style sheets don't just work on text. You also can use style sheets to control lists, tables, and images as well as text.

Style sheet specifications are set by the World Wide Web Consortium and, if you are interested, you can read the entire specification and see an example of style sheet usage at `http://w3c.org/Style/` (see Figure 20.1).

FIGURE 20.1 The W3 Consortium's Style Sheet specifications page.

Style sheets are typically saved as separate files and can be fairly complex to create from scratch. You can create your own style sheets by using FrontPage, but before you attempt it, you should read and understand the specifications for style sheets as defined by the W3 Consortium.

But there is an easier way to achieve the same results. FrontPage saves you the complexity and tedium of having to work directly with style sheets. Instead, FrontPage allows you to use what it calls *themes* to change the look-and-feel of your Webs. Themes are predefined style sheets you can use to create new Webs or that you can apply to your existing Webs.

 Even though you will most often apply themes to your entire Web, themes can also be applied to individual pages.

Figures 20.2, 20.3, and 20.4 show some examples of FrontPage themes you can apply to your Webs.

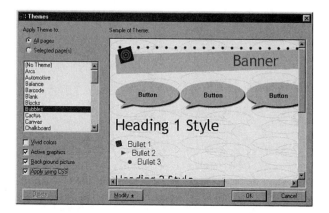

FIGURE 20.2   FrontPage's Bubbles theme.

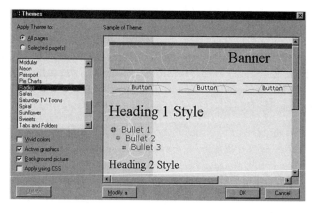

FIGURE 20.3   FrontPage's Radius theme.

FIGURE 20.4   FrontPage's Saturday TV Toons theme.

APPLYING THEMES TO YOUR WEB

If you want to apply one of FrontPage's pre-packaged themes to your
Web, or if you just want to experiment with themes to see how they look
and what effects they have, you can easily apply any or all of the accom-
panying themes. Your only limitation is that you can only apply them one
at a time.

When applying themes, it is always best to plan
before you act. In other words, it is best to look over
the available themes while you are still planning your
Web site and select the theme you think you will want
to use before you invest a lot of time and sweat in
your site. You can apply a theme to an existing site,
but sometimes a newly applied theme can make some
fairly drastic changes to your site—changes that can
result in a lot more work for you.

To apply a theme to your Web

1. Select the Web you want to apply the theme to and open the Web in FrontPage.

2. From the Format menu, select Theme to open the Themes dialog box (see Figure 20.5).

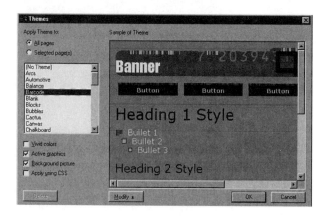

FIGURE 20.5   The FrontPage Themes dialog box.

3. To apply the theme to the entire Web, select the All Pages radio button under the Apply Theme To section. To merely apply the theme to certain page, select the Selected Page(s) radio button.

4. Scroll down through the selection of themes until you see a theme you like. As you highlight each theme, you will see a representation of the theme displayed in the Sample of Theme window on the right.

5. When you see a theme that you like, select OK, and FrontPage begins applying that theme your designated pages or Web. Depending on how many pages are being changed, this process could take anywhere from a few seconds to a few minutes.

6. When FrontPage has finished applying the new theme, your page(s) will be displayed with the new theme applied (see Figure 20.6).

FIGURE 20.6   Your Web with its new theme applied.

Even though FrontPage allows you to modify its pre-packaged themes (and the associated style sheet) to change colors, fonts, and so on, don't immediately jump right in and start making changes. Take some time to become familiar with how themes work and the underlying style sheet before you start making changes. Read over the style sheet specifications located at http://w3c.org/Style/, and make sure you have at least a rudimentary understanding of style sheets before you begin tinkering. You'll thank yourself later and avoid a mountain of potential headaches.

MODIFYING A FRONTPAGE THEME

If you are not totally satisfied with the themes Microsoft includes with FrontPage, you can always select a theme and make modifications to it.

To modify one of the existing themes

1. From the Format menu, select Themes to open the Themes dialog box (see Figure 20.7).

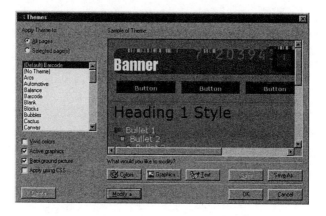

FIGURE 20.7   The Themes dialog box in FrontPage.

2. Select the theme you want to modify from the listing of available themes. The theme you select appears in the Sample of Theme window.

3. Select the Modify button and the dialog box displays three additional buttons—Colors, Graphics, and Text. Select one of these three buttons for the type of theme item you want to modify. If you want to modify one or more of the text items select the Text button. The Modify Theme dialog box displays the text items and how they are defined (see Figure 20.8).

4. From the Item dropbox, select the item you want to change. For example, if you select Heading 1, the font used for all Heading 1 headings will be displayed (see Figure 20.9).

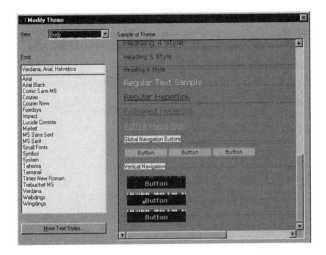

FIGURE 20.8   The Modify Theme dialog box in FrontPage displaying text items.

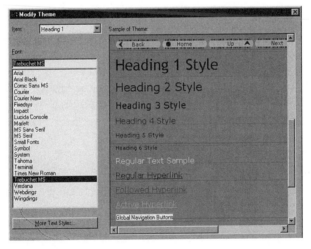

FIGURE 20.9   The Modify Theme dialog box displaying the Heading 1 font setting.

5. Select a different font for your Heading 1 settings, and the new font now defines how all Heading 1 headings will be displayed (see Figure 20.10).

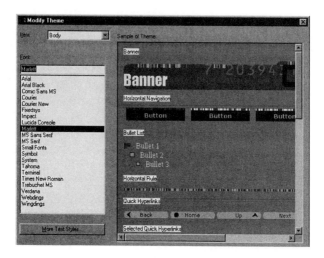

FIGURE 20.10   The Modify Theme dialog box displaying the new Heading 1 font setting.

6. If you want to change any of the other heading size settings (2–6), make those changes as you did in steps 4 and 5 and then select OK.

7. To make sure you don't overwrite the existing theme, select the Save As button and save your changes to a new theme. By default, FrontPage will offer the theme name Copy of *theme*. You can accept this suggestion or select a different name. Select OK again to close the dialog box.

In this lesson, you learned about style sheets and themes and how to apply themes to your Webs. In the next lesson, you learn how to create interactive forms on your pages.

Lesson 21

Using Forms

In this lesson, you learn how to create interactive forms on your Web pages.

Understanding Forms

Most of you have visited Web sites where you've been asked to fill out some type of onscreen form. If you've ever used a search engine, when you entered the keyword or words you wanted to search on, you filled out an onscreen form.

Forms are an interactive tool used by Web designers to gather information from users. All forms use a common set of form elements and differ mainly on what happens to the information after it is collected.

 Forms are another place where it helps to be publishing to a Web server that has the FrontPage extensions installed. While it is not absolutely essential to have FrontPage extensions installed to process forms, the extensions will help make processing forms a lot easier.

Form Elements

There are six basic form elements you use in various combinations to create your forms—a one-line text box, a scrolling text box, a check box, a radio button, a drop-down menu, and a pushbutton. What follows is an overview of each of the form elements available for you to use and what each element is used for.

ONE-LINE TEXT BOXES

A one-line text box is the simplest form element you can use in your Web page forms. A one-line text box is used when you want the user to supply a few words or perhaps one or two sentences of text (see Figure 21.1).

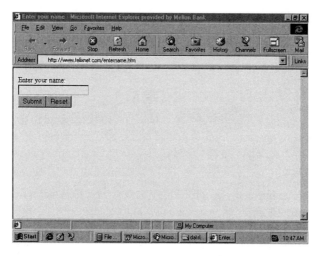

FIGURE 21.1   A one-line text box in a simple FrontPage form.

FrontPage enables you to control the width, in characters, of the text box's appearance onscreen. FrontPage also allows you to validate the information the user enters into your text box.

SCROLLING TEXT BOXES

Scrolling text boxes are nearly identical to one-line text boxes, except that scrolling text boxes can span multiple lines of text and allow you to scroll through the entered text.

CHECK BOXES

Check boxes are used when you want the user to select one or more items from a list of choices (see Figure 21.2).

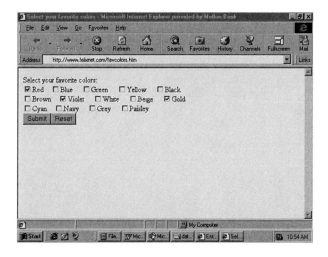

FIGURE 21.2   A selection involving check boxes.

Check boxes are literally yes/no answers. Place a check in the box, and you are answering yes. Leave the check box blank, and you are answering no to the inquiry.

RADIO BUTTONS

Radio buttons are similar to check boxes in that the user is selecting from a list of items. The difference between radio buttons and check boxes is that with radio buttons you can only select one item in the list. Radio buttons are named after the buttons that are used in car radios. Radio buttons used in forms are just like the radio buttons on car radios—they only allow you to select one option at a time (see Figure 21.3).

DROP-DOWN MENUS

Drop-down menus are another means of having the user select one item from a list of items. Typically, a drop-down menu is used in place of a collection of radio buttons when the list is extensive—having the users select what state they live in from a list of all 50 states, for example. While you could place 50 radio buttons on your form, it would be a bit cumbersome. Creating a drop-down menu containing a list of 50 states makes for a lot cleaner interface.

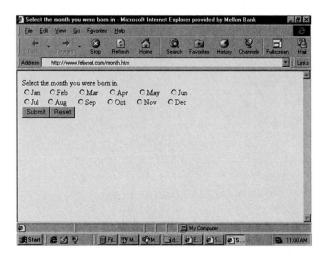

FIGURE 21.3   A selection involving radio buttons.

 You can select more than one item in a drop-down menu if you set Allow Multiple Selections to Yes in the Form Field Properties dialog box.

PUSHBUTTONS

A pushbutton is used to process some action in your form, most often either to submit the information the user has supplied for the next step in processing or simply to reset the values in the form to their initial state.

CREATING INTERACTIVE FORMS

Creating interactive forms using FrontPage is a snap but, like creating any other type of Web page, you first need to plan what type of information you want to request from those who visit your site.

One very common type of interactive form is what has been termed the *guest book*. A guest book merely asks users to enter some type of information about themselves and possibly leave a comment.

To create a guest book interactive form

   1.   Open a new blank page in FrontPage.

Even though there is a guest book template that you can use to create a guest book on your site, building one from scratch allows you to learn about creating interactive forms and allows you to create a guest book with the type of questions you want to ask your visitors.

2. Enter a sample heading, something like you see in Figure 21.4.

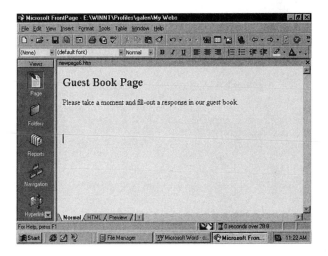

FIGURE 21.4   A sample heading you might use when creating a guest book page.

3. From the Insert menu, select Form, Form to create an empty form like you see in Figure 21.5.

 At any time, feel free to insert line breaks into your form so the form elements and text you enter are not jumbled together. This is merely for aesthetics, but it will help create a better looking page.

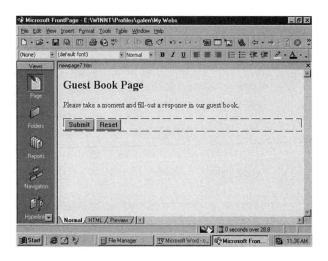

FIGURE 21.5   An empty form.

4. Inside the empty form, enter the following text:

   How did you did you find this Web site?

5. From the Insert menu, select Form, One-line Text Box to enter a one-line text box after the text you just entered.

6. Enter the following text:

   Did you find useful information on this site?

7. From the Insert menu, select Form, Radio Button to enter a radio button after the text. After the radio button, enter the following text:

   Yes

8. Repeat step 7, but after the radio button, enter the following text:

   No

9. Enter the following text:

   Comments?

10. Place your cursor below the "Comments?" text, and from the Insert menu, select Form, Scrolling Text Box. Your form should look similar to the form in Figure 21.6.

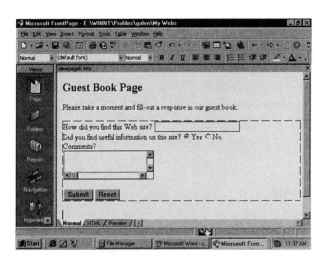

FIGURE 21.6   The completed sample guest book page.

PROCESSING FORMS WITH FRONTPAGE

The only thing left to do is decide how you want to process the information generated by your guest book page. Two easy and common choices are

- Format the information into another Web page
- Have the information emailed to you

To process the information from your form

1. Right-click anywhere inside your form and select Form Properties from the shortcut menu to open the Form Properties dialog box (see Figure 21.7).

2. By default, FrontPage processes forms information and saves it into the _private directory in the file form_results.txt. You can set FrontPage to process your forms into whatever file you choose, including an HTML file. If you want to use an HTML file, select the Options button to open the Options for Saving Results of Form dialog box (see Figure 21.8).

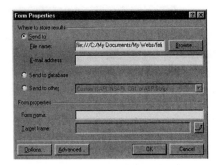

FIGURE 21.7   The Form Properties dialog box.

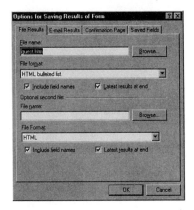

FIGURE 21.8   The Options for Saving Results of Form dialog box.

3. Enter a new filename with an .HTM or .HTML file extension. Also, select the File Format dropbox and select how you want the HTML file formatted. Select OK to exit the dialog box.

4. If you want to have the information processed and sent to you in an email message, go back to step 2, delete the filename, and enter your email address into the Email Address text box. Select OK to save and exit the dialog box.

That's it. You've created your first interactive form. All you have to do now is publish this page to your Web server. When users visit this page, they will be able to fill out your guest book (see Figure 21.9).

needs, you can still save time by using a template that is close in structure to what you are creating. Just remember, FrontPage templates are just hat, templates—flexible foundations from which you can build Web sites.

> The initial page of your Web site is typically named index.htm/.html, but not always. Depending on who is managing your Web server and what Web server software they are using, the initial page could be named default.htm/.html or home.html/.html. Make sure you check first before you publish your site to its server.

er you create your Web, you can start adding the various pages you t to see. As with any project or task, it is best to start at the beginning, ch means start with the first page visitors will see when they visit r site. From there, you can methodically work down through your site, ding the pages you need to display the information you are presenting ur site.

> Avoid using too many fonts in your site. Try to pick one or two fonts and use them consistently. While FrontPage and other Web site construction tools give you dozens of fonts you can use, using too many fonts can detract from your site's appearance and professionalism.

n't forget the multitude of tools available in FrontPage to help you ur site. You can use Image Composer to help create your images phics (see Figure 22.2), and you can use the GIF Animator to help duce any animated GIFs you might want to add to your site ure 22.3).

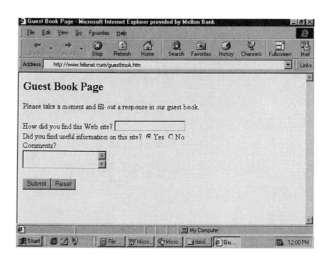

FIGURE 21.9   The sample guest book page as it will appear to visitors to your site.

Keep in mind that this is a very simple example of how you can use forms in your Web pages. Forms can be a lot more complex and can be used to process an almost unlimited amount of data including processing purchases if you want to set up a site for any type of Web commerce.

It is beyond the scope and intent of this lesson (and this book) to cover forms processing beyond this introductory example. If you want to add sophisticated forms processing to your Web pages, there are numerous books available from Sams and Macmillan Computer Publishing that can help you setup complex forms.

In this lesson, you learned how to create interactive forms in FrontPage by building a simple guest book page. In the next and final lesson, you learn how to put all of your knowledge together to build your Web site.

LESSON 22

USING FRONTPAGE FOR YOUR OWN WEB SITE

In this lesson, you learn how to create a Web site from start to finish.

DECIDING WHAT TYPE OF SITE YOU WANT TO CREATE

In the last 21 lessons, you have learned the various tasks necessary to use FrontPage to create your Web site. You have learned how to create Webs and pages, how to select themes and style sheets, how to insert images and text, and how to create frames.

Now you're going to put together all of those individual elements you've learned and create a Web site.

The first thing you need to decide is what type of site you want to create. Will it be a corporate information site? Will it be a support site for a hardware or software product you created? Or will it be a personal site you create just for the fun of it to showcase your personal accomplishments?

PLANNING YOUR SITE

Before you even turn on your PC and start FrontPage, sit down with pencil and paper and plan your site. Specify that content you want to include in your site, and map out how you want at least the top-level pages organized.

 Web sites are "works in progress," so don't can plan everything down to the smallest d work on the basis of how your site will loo rest will fall into place as you begin to wor after it has been up for a while and you'v feedback on the content.

Planning the site in advance will give you a basic bluep and save you a lot of time later.

GETTING STARTED WITH YO

Once you decide what type of site you will be constr made your basic plans using pencil and paper, it's tir FrontPage.

First, check to see if FrontPage has a template (or f templates) you can use for the underlying structure

FIGURE 22.1   FrontPage Web templates

Using a FrontPage template, both Web an you hours of tedium. Even if there isn't a

A
wa
wh
yo
bu
in y

And c
with y
and gr
you pr
(see Fi

Figure 22.2   Microsoft's Image Composer.

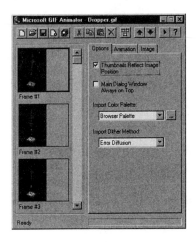

Figure 22.3   The GIF Animator application program.

But don't forget the tools in FrontPage. Don't forget you can use
FrontPage tools to add hover buttons, thumbnails, marquees, and hit counters (see Figure 22.4).

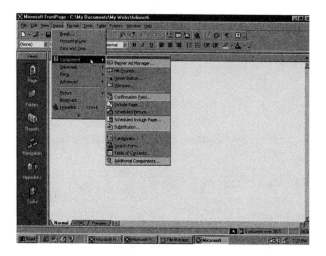

FIGURE 22.4 Some of the tools you can use in FrontPage to add features to your site.

 Don't be afraid to experiment with other tools in FrontPage if you need to simply create a new blank page to test the effect or tool with which you are experimenting.

ADDING ADDITIONAL PAGES AND DETAILS

As you add pages to your site, remember the various page templates FrontPage makes available to you (see Figure 22.5).

 You've all seen those "page under construction" graphics that seem to pop up whenever someone is building his or her site or adding pages. A word of advice—resist using them. Web sites and pages are works in progress and therefore always under construction. Using those "under construction" graphics looks amateurish.

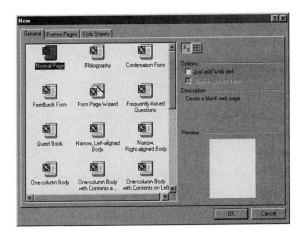

FIGURE 22.5   FrontPage's Web page templates.

PUBLISHING YOUR SITE

Once you've developed your site to a state where you think it is ready for people to start viewing it, you are ready to publish it.

Publishing your site is relatively simple, as you learned back in Lesson 17, "Publishing and Administering Your Work." But there is more to publishing than simply copying your Web to an Internet or intranet Web server.

The first thing you need to do after publishing your site to its new home is have someone else visit your site and give you feedback on his or her visit. Try to find someone who is not very experienced using a browser or the Internet to review your site. You want feedback from someone who is not very experienced because if he or she can find his or her way around, you can be fairly certain that more experienced users will be able to navigate your site as well.

Also, make sure your "Web-tester" tries most if not all of your links. You don't only want to make sure the links work (which you can test yourself) but how fast each page loads and if all of the image files associated with a specific page load correctly and without an unreasonable delay.

How long is an unreasonable delay? It's hard to quantify this term, but like former Supreme Court Justice Potter Stewart once said when asked to define obscenity, "…I know it when I see it." If your pages, and their associated image files, take too long to load, you will know it when you see it, and so will your Web-tester.

You also want your Web-tester to check for the "flow" of your Web site. Do certain pages follow a natural or logical progression, or are needed pages hard to find? Remember, you are posting information on your site and you want visitors to find it.

But easily finding the information on your site is of no consequence if visitors can't find your site!

Don't forget to advertise.

If you are preparing a corporate intranet site, check to see if there is any type of corporate-wide newsletter you can use to let your fellow employees know about your site. You might also want to see if your company has any type of internal newspaper. If so, volunteer to write an article about your site. Editors are always looking for ways to fill an internal newsletter or newspaper.

If your site is on the Internet, make sure you register your site with all of the major search engines—AltaVista, Lycos, Yahoo!, InfoSeek, Excite, HotBot, and WebCrawler just to name a few.

Most if not all of these search engines have a procedure and a mechanism in place for you to submit your site for entry into their database or review by their editors. Take advantage of their generosity. Don't wait for them to find you.

Here's how to add your site to Lycos:

1. Start your Web browser and go to Lycos' home page, `http://www.lycos.com`.

2. Scroll down to the bottom of the page and select the link Add Your Site to Lycos (see Figure 22.6).

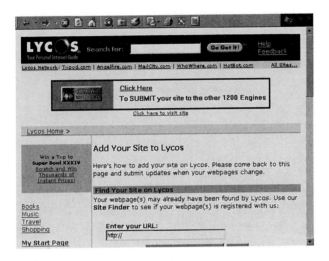

FIGURE 22.6   Adding your site to Lycos' database.

3. If your site has been on the Internet for a few weeks, it's possible that Lycos may already have found it and entered its address in its database. You can check to see if your site is already listed by using the Find Your Site on Lycos form. Enter the URL of your site and select the Find URL on Lycos button.

4. If you are just now publishing your site, select the Add Your Site Now form. Enter your site's URL and enter your email address so Lycos can send you confirmation of the entry.

5. Select the Add Site to Lycos button and you're done.

If you're not sure where or how to find other Internet search engines, you can find a fairly substantial list at http://www.sixnet.com (The Portal @ FelixNet.Com). There is a section near the top of the page labeled Search Engines that lists all of the major Internet search engines and probably a few you've never heard of (see Figure 22.7).

FIGURE 22.7   The Portal @ FelixNet.Com located at
`http://www.felixnet.com`.

In this lesson, you learned how to use FrontPage to create your site from stem to stern. Congratulations, you've completed *Sams Teach Yourself Microsoft FrontPage 2000 in 10 Minutes*. You should now feel pretty comfortable using FrontPage to create Web sites and modify Web pages. Even though you've completed all of the lessons, you might find it handy to keep this text nearby to use as a quick reference while you continue to use FrontPage on the sites you build.

INDEX

FrontPage 2000

Web site at:
http://www.fp2k.com

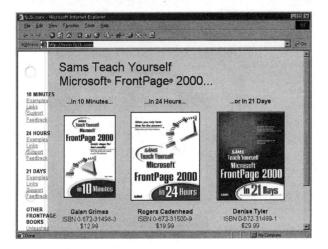

Here you'll find:

- **Example files:** Some of the examples—complete with graphics and media files—will be available online

- **Updated links to the sites mentioned in the book:** If a site has moved elsewhere, we'll update it here

- **Answers to reader questions:** Questions that aren't already covered in the book's Q&A sections

- **Corrections and clarifications:** When errors are brought to our attention, they'll be described on the site with the corrected text and any other material that's relevant